JUST -IN- TIME

The Future of Enablement in a World of AI

BY MELANIE FELLAY

CEO OF SPEKIT

"Mel has an uncanny ability to work in any role or department, spot the bottlenecks and come up with ideas for improvement. Her deep experience and impressive accomplishments at RealtyShares and growing Spekit over the last eight years have yielded unique insights that make her the perfect person to write this book!"

NAV ATHWAL, Managing Director Terra Ag Ventures, former CEO RealtyShares

"If you're an enablement leader or sales leader who wants to understand the challenges impacting enablement, why the current technology stack isn't helping, and what to do about it, you need to read this book. Mel's journey highlights many practical tips and shares the solution she found in Just-In-Time Enablement."

JOHN BARROWS, CEO John Barrows

Just-In-Time: The Future of Enablement in a World of AI is published by Spekit.
Author: Melanie Fellay | Editor: Kelly Kearsley | Designer: Jenny Lee

Copyright © 2025 Spekit, Inc. All rights reserved.

https://spekit.com/

Table of Contents

Introduction: The elevator pitch	1
Chapter 1: Broken enablement	9
Chapter 2: The fragmented enablement landscape	19
Chapter 3: The answer: Just-In-Time Enablement	47
Chapter 4: Just-In-Time Enablement is contextual	55
Chapter 5: Just-In-Time Enablement is personalized	69
Chapter 6: Just-In-Time Enablement is simple	83
Chapter 7: The future of content is unified	97
Chapter 8: The future of content is dynamic	113
Chapter 9: The future of content is measurable	135
Chapter 10: Preparing for the future	149
Conclusion	169

INTRODUCTION
The elevator pitch

I'm not your typical tech founder: I don't write code.

I also don't have a long career or a degree in education, enablement, or instructional design. Yet, here I am, leading a company that's revolutionizing how teams enable their employees.

So, how did I get here? And why have I dedicated the past eight years of my career to solving this problem?

We have entered what I call the Change Economy. The rise of artificial intelligence (AI) is accelerating innovation at an unprecedented rate. Technological advancement is pushing the pace of business beyond anything we've seen before, transforming how we build, prospect, sell, connect with and service customers.

This fast-moving and hyper-competitive environment demands a radical shift in how we think and operate. What worked yesterday won't cut it tomorrow.

In fact, 42% of CEOs say that their companies will remain viable for less than ten years if they don't make significant changes[1]. And, unfortunately, I've seen firsthand what happens when organizations fall behind: they become slow and, ultimately, go extinct. I'll share that story shortly.

Sales teams must evolve to thrive in this new reality. But they can't do it alone. They need enablement, but not the kind they've relied on in the past. The old playbooks, the annual training programs, the outdated content libraries, and the reactive approach to enablement are all quickly becoming liabilities.

Somewhere along the way, we overcomplicated things and got lost in the endless sea of software categories, features, methodologies, frameworks, and titles. That's why defining enablement has been so hard.

So, for the purposes of this book, I define enablement as:

> **en·a·ble·ment** *noun*
> /iˈnāb(ə)lmənt/
>
> The process of helping a rep be able to sell.

This definition gets to the heart of what enablement is all about. It became my guiding principle as I set out to reimagine how to empower our sales team. It's also the definition I'll use throughout this book.

This increasing pace of change is why I felt compelled to write this book *now*.

Sales teams need a fresh approach to enablement—one that embraces speed, agility, and continuous learning in the age of AI.

---

[1] "PwC's 28th Annual Global CEO Survey" 2025; https://www.pwc.com/gx/en/issues/c-suite-insights/ceo-survey.html

This book is a deep dive into the future of enablement, fueled by research, hard data and hundreds of conversations with those on the front lines, including sales leaders, executives, reps, enablement practitioners, and peers.

Inside, you'll find practical strategies, real-world insights, and the tools you need to succeed in this new era. Nearly every chapter also provides Pro Tips within the content—in context—so that you can learn a concept and instantly find practical recommendations for applying it in real-world scenarios.

My hope is that this book resonates with enablement professionals, go-to-market (GTM) leaders, and executives alike. While all chapters explore the future of enablement and the role of AI, in some we'll dive more deeply into practical implementation than others. The chapter highlights will help you quickly understand the content of each chapter and identify what's most relevant to your needs.

I've also included personal stories throughout this book, such as the challenges that sparked the idea for Spekit and my experience at a previous fast-growing startup. Why? Because sometimes, the best way to learn is through others' painful experiences. But the other reason, honestly, is because I've lost count of the number of business books I stopped reading before getting to Chapter Three because they simply didn't engage me, so my hope is that these anecdotes make the important story I'm telling that much more engaging.

Let's dive in, starting with the question: How did this quest for a better approach to enablement start in the first place?

A fateful Slack message

It all began with a simple Slack message in October 2017 when I worked at RealtyShares, then a promising real estate crowdfunding platform.

"Meet me by the elevators."

It wasn't exactly a line out of a Hollywood script, but it marked the true beginning of Spekit.

I had recently learned that Zari Zahra, a RealtyShares product manager, had resigned. I was in shock. I knew Zari was incredibly talented and that losing her, and everything she knew about the product's inner workings, would be a huge blow to the team.

I didn't know her well, but I agreed with almost everything she said every time we were in meetings together - she just "got it." I assumed part of the reason she was leaving was because she was burnt out, and our conversation confirmed it.

But amid my initial surprise, a door of opportunity creaked open. This was my chance to pitch my vision for a solution to one of the problems that contributed to Zari's departure. So, I sent her that fateful Slack message.

I'd been thinking about my idea constantly; I even had early product designs in the product design tool, Sketch (RIP). However, I wasn't sure what to do with the idea—I wasn't sure I wanted to start a company, and I didn't want to appear distracted from my RealtyShares work. I loved my job and had been granted many growth opportunities, most recently being promoted to chief of staff to our new chief executive officer (CEO).

But with Zari's pending departure, there was little to lose. So there, by the elevator, I relayed to her my vision for what would later become our company.

At first, Zari assumed I was describing an existing enablement tool.

"**Let's buy it,**" Zari declared after hearing my pitch.

Confused, I asked, "Buy what?"

"The tool you just described," she clarified. "We desperately need something like that."

"No, Zari, you don't understand. This tool I'm describing doesn't exist. I'm suggesting we build it."

"Oh wow, okay… Well, I'm flying to Fiji next week for some time off, but let me think about it," Zari replied.

Standing by those elevators on our way back up to the office, with a mix of apprehension and excitement, I knew I had found the perfect partner.

I knew she would take some convincing and some of her own research to validate the opportunity, but I had a strong feeling she would come around. And she did, just a week later, sending me her first iterations of our logo designs from her hotel room.

With Zari's product management expertise and my vision, I knew we were onto something game-changing—the catalyst for a learning revolution.

We envisioned a product that would revolutionize how employees learn and access information, leading to increased productivity and, ultimately, faster growth.

This was the birth of Spekit and the start of a journey that would challenge and transform the way businesses approach enablement.

A better way: Just-In-Time Enablement

I was fresh faced and full of optimism (and a healthy dose of anxiety) as we prepared to take a giant leap of faith. Little did I know that the coming years for us as first-time entrepreneurs would include a global pandemic, a remote work revolution, and a tech boom followed by a sobering recession.

Through it all, we held onto a vision: a world where employees effortlessly master their ever-changing roles.

A world where each and every employee thrives, learning and finding content and answers, precisely when and where they need it.

We called this concept **Just-In-Time Enablement**.

Just-In-Time Enablement

1. Encompasses the various methods for integrating learning and Enablement in the Flow of Work™.

2. Ensures reps know what they need to know, when and where they need to know it.

Just-In-Time Enablement isn't just another buzzword. It represents a revolutionary yet practical, science-based approach to mastering new skills and knowledge, built off of decades of learning research by pioneering psychologists, leadership researchers, and workforce productivity experts.

But while the promise of Just-In-Time Enablement remains incredible, a significant challenge threatens to derail the opportunity: **content decay**.

During the last eight years of researching this problem, I've spoken with leaders at thousands of companies. Every single team reported that keeping content fresh, accurate, and up to date was a massive challenge, despite the plethora of solutions they've tried, from content audits to expiration dates. Outdated information kills trust with reps and leaders alike, can damage the customer experience, and overwhelms enablement teams.

The good news? AI is here to help and this book explores how AI can transform and automate content curation to finally solve the "messy content" problem. Manual content management will soon be a relic of the past.

This future is now

Everything we read about AI and the future isn't far-off science fiction; it's on the horizon or already happening.

Join me as we explore this exciting new era of information and discover how AI can transform your enablement program. Read to learn more about:

- **The urgent need for change:** The widening gap between traditional enablement methods and the urgent demands of today's business environment.

- **The power and science of Just-In-Time Enablement:** The science of how the brain processes information, revealing why delivering the right resources at the right time drives peak performance, accelerates learning, and drives business growth.

- **The future of rep enablement:** A world where enablement is contextual, personalized, and simple and every rep has their very own AI-powered enablement assistant providing tailored coaching and content, simplifying learning, and freeing up more time to sell.

- **The future of content:** The challenges of content curation and decay and the opportunity to harness AI to create a unified, dynamic, and measurable content ecosystem full of powerful insights.

The future belongs to those who can adapt, and adapt quickly. So buckle up and get ready to unlock the full potential of your reps.

CHAPTER 1

Broken enablement

HIGHLIGHTS ─────────────────────

Explore how AI, globalization, and economic shifts are accelerating the rate of innovation, forcing businesses to cultivate learning agility—or risk extinction.

Learn from a real-world case study of a disastrous customer relationship management system (CRM) implementation and the surprising lessons it revealed about enablement.

Discover the consequences of ineffective enablement, from missed sales targets to costly mistakes and eroded customer trust.

Uncover the common enablement challenges plaguing organizations of all sizes, including ineffective onboarding, knowledge chaos, and poor accountability.

As a CEO, one thing keeps me up at night: the fear of falling behind. Not innovating quickly enough, missing our goals, and not keeping up with the opportunities that AI presents.

I know I'm not alone. Salesforce's 2024 State of Sales report confirms this:

- 78% of sales leaders are concerned that their companies are missing out on generative AI.
- 57% of organizations think competition has gotten trickier than last year.
- 67% of sales reps don't expect to meet their quotas this year, and 84% missed it last year.[1]

In this Change Economy, CEOs and leadership teams everywhere are feeling the pressure to adapt at lightning speed to technological advancements, globalization, and economic shifts. In the current hypercompetitive environment, organizations that struggle to keep pace become yesterday's news.

But it's about more than missing out on AI opportunities or delaying product launches. It's the constant pressure to learn from mistakes and make tough decisions in a rapidly changing environment. One of the reasons why I love technology is that it embodies this increasing rate of change. Remember bulky software discs and yearly updates? Today, software updates happen in real time, every minute of every day.

With the rise of AI, change is happening faster than ever. The timeline from being the latest, hottest technology on the market to being a commodity is decreasing by the day. Take a look at Conversation Intelligence (CI) technology pioneered by organizations like Gong. This

---

[1] Salesforce. State of Sales Report. 2024. Available at: https://www.salesforce.com/resources/research-reports/state-of-sales/ © 2024 Salesforce, Inc. All rights reserved.

category of software was the hottest new technology on the block seven years ago, but fast forward to today, and CI is no longer revolutionary; it's a table-stakes feature in any call-recording or video conferencing software, including Zoom or Teams.

We're all racing against the clock. Automation is no longer a futuristic fantasy. Routine tasks are being replaced by robotic efficiency, creating entirely new roles and responsibilities. The half-life of skills is shrinking at an alarming rate. What was valuable today might be obsolete next year. This constant need to adapt demands **learning agility**: the ability to rapidly acquire and apply new knowledge and skills as challenges and opportunities morph around you.

Without this ability, you risk falling behind—or failing altogether.

Buckling under growth

I've seen the risk of falling behind firsthand.

I forged my vision for enablement in the fires of a fast-growing technology company struggling to keep pace.

RealtyShares was a real estate crowdfunding platform that had raised $60 million from top venture firms like Menlo Ventures, Union Square Ventures, and General Catalyst. The premise was simple: connect individual accredited investors with interesting real estate investment opportunities. However, the execution of the idea was very complex.

I joined the company shortly after their Series A in 2015 as the 20th employee. My first title was investor services associate, but the role would best be described as a full-cycle customer manager. I answered thousands of customers' inquiries while helping them onboard and learn about our new listings. I wasn't on the job for two weeks before my manager quit, and I had no option but to figure it out. After building the investor services team and establishing systems and processes for other departments, I transitioned into the role of business operations, combining elements of process, technology, and data with sprinkles of product management.

By the end of 2016, the company had grown to more than 150 employees. The modern workplace was also undergoing a seismic shift with the rise of Software as a Service (SaaS) solutions for everything. "Digital transformation" was the new buzzword, but many companies, including ours, struggled to keep up with the daily workload.

We had a visionary CEO and team, but we were missing our goals, and our productivity was suffering. We were doing everything we could to drive revenue. But despite our rapid growth in employee count, it felt like we were moving more slowly than ever. All of this was causing an environment riddled with super slow decision-making, mistakes, and tons of frustration—on top of an already challenging, ambitious vision.

A failed CRM system

Our Salesforce implementation was the straw that broke the camel's back. Despite hundreds of hours of planning and spending nearly $1 million on headcount, implementation fees, and licenses, the end result resembled a Rube Goldberg machine: overly complex.

Thanks to the poor user experience we'd designed, we had terrible adoption, and therefore, we weren't getting any of the numerous benefits that CRMs offer, like more visibility into our pipeline and data to understand our business. Instead, we were more in the dark than ever. Even working in Excel and with our older, basic CRM felt more manageable at that point.

Our implementation of Salesforce was failing to meet our needs and became a source of frustration and inefficiency for everyone involved, especially our CEO.

One evening, our CEO approached me with a desperate solution: "Mel, I think we should get rid of Salesforce and build our own internal platform. Our business is too complex."

I was puzzled. I hadn't been involved in our Salesforce implementation and had never managed a CRM before, **but I knew our challenges weren't due to the Salesforce platform itself—they were an "us" problem**. Building something from scratch would only distract our engineers from innovating our actual platform to solve our customers' needs.

I pointed out the window to the massive Salesforce tower under construction two blocks away in the heart of San Francisco. "They seem to have something figured out," I suggested. "Let me take a closer look before we invest in building our own CRM."

During the next few months, I took ownership of our Salesforce platform, determined to fix the issues. It turns out that improving the platform's usability with system design configurations, adding some light automation, and simplifying page layouts were the easy parts.

Unfortunately, I quickly realized our problems ran much deeper than our clunky implementation.

Battling goldfish memory

The depth of our challenges became glaringly evident during a crucial revenue forecasting meeting with our executive team just before a critical board meeting. We needed accurate data to understand our financial health and projections clearly. But as we started diving into the numbers, disaster unfolded.

Turns out, each of our sales leaders at the time, and their respective teams, had a different interpretation of our deal stages. As a result, the pipeline data that I'd spent hours compiling and that I had added to our board deck was pretty much useless. It wasn't a good look for any of us. Our CEO was furious, and reasonably so.

I was frustrated because it wasn't for lack of trying. I had sent countless emails, organized lunch-and-learn sessions, and even created a comprehensive 50-page Salesforce training manual (complete with detailed deal stage definitions buried deep on page 17).

But alas, we had a collective case of **goldfish memory**. Our employees forgot new information within seconds of hearing or reading it, and everything we did to address it wasn't working.

No amount of CRM optimization could compensate for a fundamental lack of knowledge, process adherence, and consistent execution.

But was it really their fault?

We had, as I later discovered, an **enablement problem**.

The challenges of enablement

Back in 2017, the role or department of sales enablement was still a relatively new concept for many companies, but it was becoming more common.

While we had a human resources (HR) team that handled some learning and development (L&D) responsibilities, a dedicated enablement team was unheard of in the vast majority of organizations. To be honest, I hadn't encountered the term until I started researching ways to address our growing pains.

But the enablement struggle was—and seemingly remains—ubiquitous. Looking back after eight years of research and countless conversations with business leaders, I realize that many organizations have accepted these challenges and the consequences of ineffective enablement as an unavoidable reality.

But it doesn't have to be that way.

The more I spent time researching these problems, the more I realized that they weren't just the challenges we faced at RealtyShares; almost every friend or peer I spoke to at other companies were facing them too (and still do today!). Here's a glimpse into those common pain points and the ripple effects they create across an organization.

Expensive, slow onboarding

New hires were drowning in an endless stream of information about our industry, products, services, jargon, regulations, policies, processes, sales playbooks, pricing models, platforms, features, internal tools, and external tools—all without proper documentation or training.

The onboarding process at RealtyShares was incredibly manual, relying heavily on already overwhelmed managers. We even had new employees, just weeks into the job, training even newer hires because they were the only ones who knew how to do certain things. Our top performers were spending more time onboarding than selling, which was a drain on our resources (and revenue)!

This onboarding experience wasn't unique to us. Many companies lack thoughtful onboarding programs. When onboarding is inefficient and disorganized, new hires take longer to ramp up and contribute to revenue generation, leading to missed sales targets or delayed project timelines. In a world where speed is the advantage, speed of ramp is essential.

Ineffective change management

Even if someone successfully navigated the onboarding maze, our rapidly changing industry, with its constant influx of new regulations and competitor activity, made it nearly impossible to keep reps updated.

We tried everything: email updates, lunch-and-learn sessions, even those dreaded, lengthy training manuals. But it was like trying to fill a sieve. The information would slip through the cracks, leaving our team confused and unprepared.

This failure to manage change effectively can quietly hurt revenue streams. Ineffective change management creates a ripple effect of inefficiency and missed opportunities. When employees are unsure of the latest processes or lack the knowledge to adapt to new information, their productivity and ability to drive new revenue suffer, and so does your customer experience. There's nothing worse than getting on a call with your vendor's customer success manager and realizing that they don't know about the latest feature in the platform you're trying to get help with. But with the pace of innovation and scattered product knowledge, can we really blame them?

Knowledge chaos, reduced productivity

The constant changes and barrage of communications created a state of perpetual disruption. Employees were overwhelmed with information, struggling to keep up, and constantly confused.

Even when we had documentation, our reps didn't know where to find it. Was it in Google Drive or Confluence? Or, perhaps, was it buried in an email?

And if reps *did* find documentation, it was often out of date. Constant questions flooded across our office, email, Google Chat, and new communication chat tool, Slack.

As we'll explore later, the constant context switching and mental overload described above wreak havoc on team productivity. Employees waste so much time searching for answers and navigating a fragmented information landscape. When reps can't find the information they need, sales cycles and proposals stall, and opportunities slip away.

Costly mistakes

With information scattered across various platforms and minimal documentation, mistakes were inevitable. One particularly memorable incident involved a new hire who accidentally clicked the "credit" button instead of the "debit" button in our platform, resulting in an erroneous $10,000 credit to a customer's account.

We were able to retrieve the funds, but not without a lot of work and a little embarrassment. The incident highlighted the very real financial risks associated with poor enablement.

Without clear guidance and easy access to information, employees are more prone to errors. These sorts of missteps and inconsistencies damage brand reputation and erode customer trust, leading to potential churn and lost revenue opportunities.

Poor accountability

When mistakes happened, like the $10,000 credit mishap, we struggled to pinpoint the root cause. Was it a lack of skill (had we made it easy for them to master their role?) or a lack of will (had they simply not bothered to seek support)? But the real question was: how could we blame employees for errors when we hadn't provided them with the knowledge and tools they needed to succeed?

Without simple, effective enablement and clear visibility into whether employees had engaged with the resources, it was difficult to assess performance accurately or hold anyone accountable. We were operating in a black box, unable to diagnose the true drivers of behavior and performance.

Flying blind

The disastrous forecasting meeting highlighted one of the most critical consequences of our broken enablement—we couldn't trust our data. When we introduced new processes, they had abysmal adoption rates.

If they did get adopted, it wasn't much better—each manager created their own definition of the documented data. For example, one team would enter the amount of a deal as the value of a contract, while another team would include the value of the contract and the services. The inconsistencies made it incredibly difficult to diagnose our problems' root causes and both team and individual performance. *We were missing our goals, but we couldn't determine why.*

Inconsistent processes lead to inconsistent execution. Deals slowly drift away, opportunities slip through the cracks, revenue projections become unreliable, and even worse, you can't rely on your data to determine the cause.

The ticking clock

Finally, **we were running out of time**. RealtyShares wasn't profitable yet, and we needed to demonstrate real growth and innovation to secure our next round of financing. We needed our CEO to be 100% focused on finding our path to profitability, but the internal chaos and inability to trust our data were holding him back.

Faced with these mounting challenges, I knew we couldn't continue down this path. I began searching for a solution to break the knowledge chaos cycle and empower our team to thrive. Through countless conversations with peers and leaders at other companies, one thing became abundantly clear: **we weren't alone**.

This realization fueled my determination to find a better way.

CHAPTER 2

The fragmented enablement landscape

HIGHLIGHTS

Navigate the chaotic landscape of enablement solutions and uncover the pros and cons of various approaches.

Discover how this fragmented approach is failing both reps and companies and why traditional platforms struggle to keep pace with today's rapid rate of change.

Learn why flashy features often distract from the core issues of content discovery and decay, hindering true enablement success.

Explore the surprising similarities among distinct enablement solutions and the core **content engine** that drives them all.

My professional background wasn't in learning or knowledge management, which meant that the landscape of enablement technologies was utterly new to me. I didn't have a predetermined set of tools or a bias toward any particular solution.

The only non-negotiable was that the solution had to be incredibly user friendly for our users, and it also had to be super easy for my team that would need to administer the solution. Anything complex or cumbersome would be dead on arrival—our team wouldn't use it.

I approached the problem from a first-principles mindset and came to a simple goal for a solution: **Make sure every employee knows what they need to know, when and where they need to know it**.

Simple enough, right?

The chaotic alphabet soup

My journey into the world of enablement began with a deep dive into existing solutions. Google searches for "employee training magic bullet" yielded four distinct answers: Learning Management Systems (LMS), Content Management Systems (CMS), Knowledge Management Systems (KMS), and Digital Adoption Platforms (DAP)—a chaotic alphabet soup.

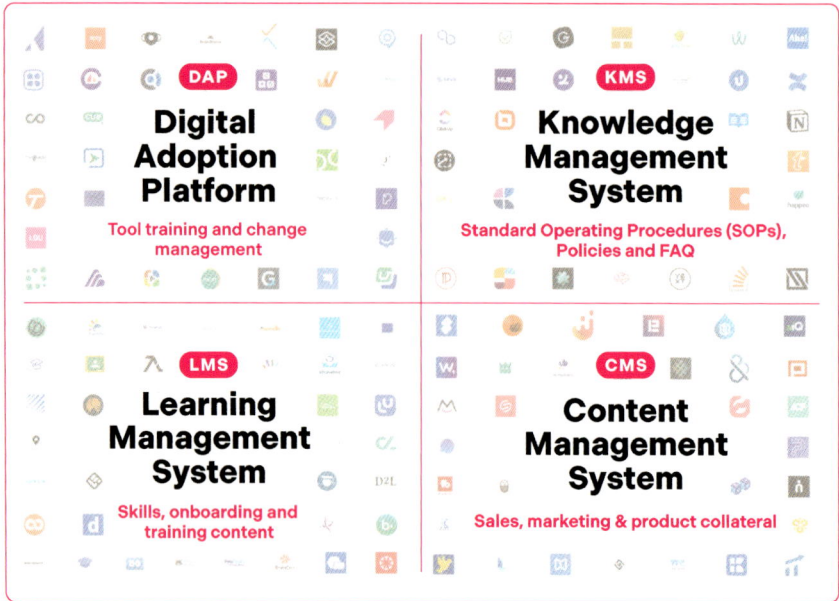

Oh, and each category of software had dozens, if not hundreds, of options. To put it into perspective, G2 currently lists more than 590 results for their "Corporate Learning Management System[2]" software category.

Each category promised to solve a piece of the puzzle, but none seemed to address the challenge holistically. This fragmentation was a red flag from the start. The idea of forcing our employees to navigate not one, but *four* separate systems to access the information they needed was nothing short of ludicrous.

Why did we need four systems—LMS, CMS, KMS, and DAP—to achieve a single objective: knowledge mastery?

I embarked on a thorough evaluation exploring over 20 different platforms. In this chapter I'll walk through the different categories of enablement software I explored, including new ones that have emerged on the market.

---

2 G2. Best Corporate Learning Management Systems. Available at: https://www.g2.com/categories/corporate-learning-management-systems

Digital Adoption Platforms

Digital Adoption Platform (DAP) *noun*

Software that is layered on top of another software product to help facilitate proficiency by guiding users through key tasks.[3]

The first category of solutions I explored was the newest: Digital Adoption Platforms (DAP).

The concept of embedding training directly inside Salesforce made a lot of sense to me. Why wouldn't that information live where our teams worked instead of buried in Google Drive?

---

3   Pendo. Digital Adoption Platform. Available at: https://www.pendo.io/glossary/digital-adoption-platform/

Designed to promote digital dexterity

DAPs promise to promote technology adoption and drive an organization's **digital dexterity** by providing guided walkthroughs, tooltips, and other features to employees directly within the tools themselves.

Digital dexterity refers to employees' ability and ambition to fully leverage existing and emerging technologies to drive business outcomes.

This concept resonated with me, given that I was working with employees from an industry (real estate), with limited technology use, and I needed to find ways to help them embrace new tools and adapt to digital changes.

Early DAPs emerged around 2011. A vendor's product and engineering teams purchased and built these DAP platforms into their software. Rather than reinventing the wheel and creating tooltips for each of their respective products, product and engineering teams utilized these DAP platforms to guide users, track usage analytics, and collect user feedback. This guidance was often very high level, focused on first-time user experiences and new feature updates.

Eventually, these vendors repurposed this same technology for internal use: guiding employees on internal tools. The logic was straightforward: if it could train end-users on a vendor's platform, why not use it to train employees on platforms like Salesforce?

Unfortunately, this approach falls short for several reasons. Some of these were immediately clear during my DAP evaluations, while others I've come to understand more deeply through supporting customers on their enablement journeys.

Designed by technical teams for technical teams

First, these DAP platforms were incredibly technical and complex, with cumbersome admin experiences. During free trials, it became clear to me that these products were initially designed for technical teams. As a result, Information Technology (IT) teams were their primary buyers. Today, some of these technologies even include capabilities like robotic process automation (RPA) and data validation, which may appeal to those buyers and are interesting technologies, but aren't enablement focused.

We needed a solution that empowered us to own the process, not one that created dependencies on external teams or complex configurations.

Most DAP platforms rely heavily on technical resources, requiring knowledge of JavaScript or other coding languages for implementation.

This simply wasn't feasible for our budget or team. Alternatively, we could rely on the vendor's services teams, which is a significant part of their business model. Still, I knew that relying on an external team for every change would be unsustainable, especially given the fragile nature of these platforms

While they had some exciting change management capabilities for alerting users of changes, the irony was that change management within the tool proved difficult. Even a minor change to an application like Salesforce, such as renaming a field or adjusting a page layout, could break the guidance and require intervention from the vendor's professional services team. This constant maintenance would quickly become a headache, especially given our rapid pace of change.

While DAPs have made strides in usability since this initial evaluation, they often remain complex solutions requiring significant technical expertise.

DAPs solve only one piece of the enablement puzzle

Putting some of the technical complexities aside, I also quickly realized that DAPs solve only one piece of the enablement puzzle. They focus too narrowly on adoption as a UX issue—rather than a knowledge issue—likely stemming from their roots of selling to product teams.

Most DAP features specifically help with guiding someone through how to navigate a tool, assuming that this alone equates to successful adoption. But our reps' needs went far beyond understanding how to click the right buttons.

We had customized our CRM to our unique business processes; the two were practically intertwined (as is the case for most businesses). For example, creating an "Opportunity" in Salesforce meant more than just filling out a form. Our reps were essentially underwriting real estate investment opportunities, with complex fields like "Loan-to-Cost Ratio" and "Loan Grade" being used to determine if a loan was approved.

Our reps needed to understand our loan underwriting policies and the meaning of each field to perform their jobs effectively. The problem? These policies were buried in a likely outdated, 80-page loan servicing manual hidden deep within Google Drive.

Furthermore, because our loan underwriting process resided in Salesforce, they also needed to master the platform and user experience.

Mastery of both was essential for leveraging our Opportunity data for reliable forecasting.

Addressing both issues required embedding the necessary knowledge—such as the loan servicing guidelines mentioned above—directly into their workflow.

We needed more than a simple plugin providing basic navigation tooltips.

"Digital adoption" is the wrong goal

Ultimately, I concluded that the focus on "digital adoption" was misplaced.

While adoption metrics are important, they often distract from the true objective: enabling reps to succeed in their roles and win business. Salesforce, or any CRM, is simply a tool—a means to an end, not the end goal itself. My goal wasn't simply "Salesforce adoption"; it was to empower our reps to master their jobs, ultimately driving increased revenue, improved productivity, and better business outcomes.

My initial excitement about DAPs stemmed from their potential to address our CRM challenges. However, I quickly realized they fell short of our broader needs, such as comprehensive sales training and a centralized content repository. More importantly, I came to believe the prevalent messaging around adoption itself was flawed (likely a product of effective marketing).

True adoption would come not from focusing on the platform itself, but on the people using it and the resources they need to succeed. Our priority had to be enabling our reps to achieve their goals as easily and effectively as possible.

PROS
- Embedded in the flow of work
- In-app change management

CONS
- Technical product that's difficult to implement and maintain
- Narrow focus on tool navigation

WHAT'S NEW
- Improved admin: less technical
- AI + federated search

How could we motivate data entry by providing immediate value, rather than making it feel like a forced chore? Embedding battlecards next to a competitive field, for example, is far more helpful to sellers preparing for competitive calls than a validation rule requiring competitor selection (and subsequent navigation guidance) before advancing to the next stage.

If our employees felt supported and had the resources they needed readily available, platform adoption would naturally follow as a *result*, not a target.

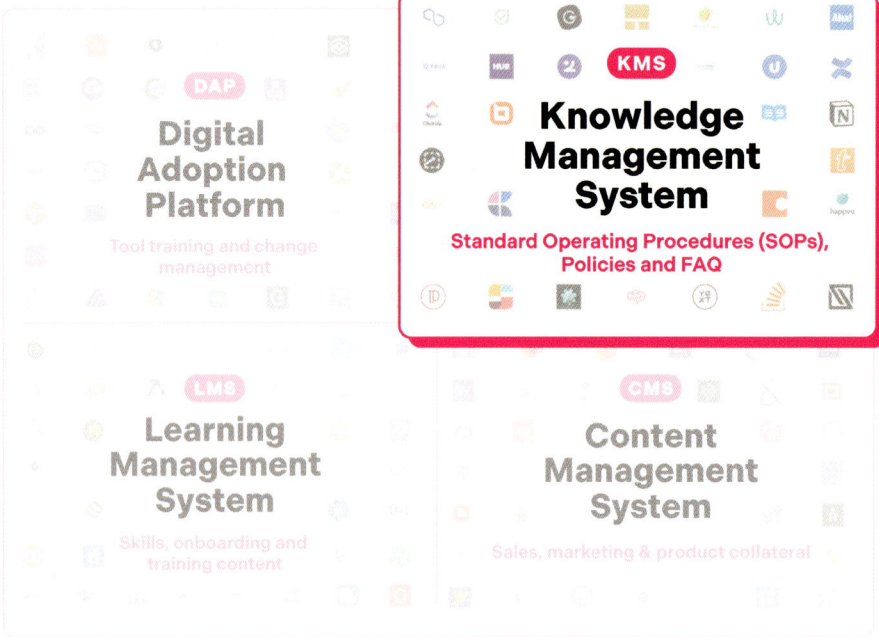

Knowledge Management Systems

Recognizing the limitations of DAPs, I turned my attention to KMSs.

> **Knowledge Management System (KMS)** *noun*
> A software platform used to centralize, capture, store, and share organizational knowledge.

Our research and development teams were using Confluence, our existing knowledge management solution that was integrated with Jira (a popular product management software), but it was also made available company wide. While functional, we found Confluence to be cumbersome and difficult to search at the time, making it less than ideal for the rest of the company—especially our sales reps, who needed to find answers as quickly as possible.

As I explored further, I realized that the user experience (UX) wasn't a Confluence-specific problem. I was struck by how outdated most KMS platforms looked and felt. Many seemed stuck in the 1990s, with clunky interfaces and confusing navigation. UX had clearly taken a backseat in these systems' development.

This was a real concern. If our employees found the knowledge base difficult to use, they simply wouldn't use it. No matter how comprehensive or well organized the content, a poor UX would undermine adoption and defeat the purpose of a centralized knowledge platform. Luckily, most KMS platforms today have AI search and answers, eliminating the need for navigation for the most part.

The one additional benefit that KMS platforms offered that I hadn't seen in DAP platforms was basic governance capabilities, notably expiration dates and verification features. That said, I don't think those do much to solve content decay, but I'll save that for Chapter Eight.

Knowing the "how" and the "why"

I noticed a trend where some of the newer KMS platforms were leveraging Chrome extensions to make their knowledge base searchable in a sidebar in any web-based application. This reminded me of the contextual promise of DAPs. Both were aimed at providing just-in-time support and guidance, but they approached this from different angles.

DAPs focused on interactive walkthroughs within applications, while this KMS approach offered a searchable knowledge base accessible from any webpage.

I thought, what if we could combine the strengths of both approaches? Imagine a solution that provides interactive guidance within applications and seamlessly integrates with a comprehensive knowledge base. This would empower employees with the "how-to" knowledge of a DAP and the deeper "why" information, all within their natural workflow.

The need for more versatile content support

This vision of a unified solution drove my continued search for a platform that could bridge the gap between DAPs and KMS, offering a comprehensive approach to knowledge management and enablement. But there was one criteria that neither platform seemed to solve for at the time: we needed a solution that could accommodate the wide range of content formats used in our daily operations.

PROS
- Searchability
- Governance features

CONS
- Clunky user experience
- Limited content support (no files)

WHAT'S NEW
- AI federated search/answers

As a real estate company, we relied on various content formats, including Portable Document Formats (PDFs), presentations, and property overviews. While KMS platforms were suitable for documenting internal policies and procedures, they lacked the ability to effectively manage and share these diverse file types.

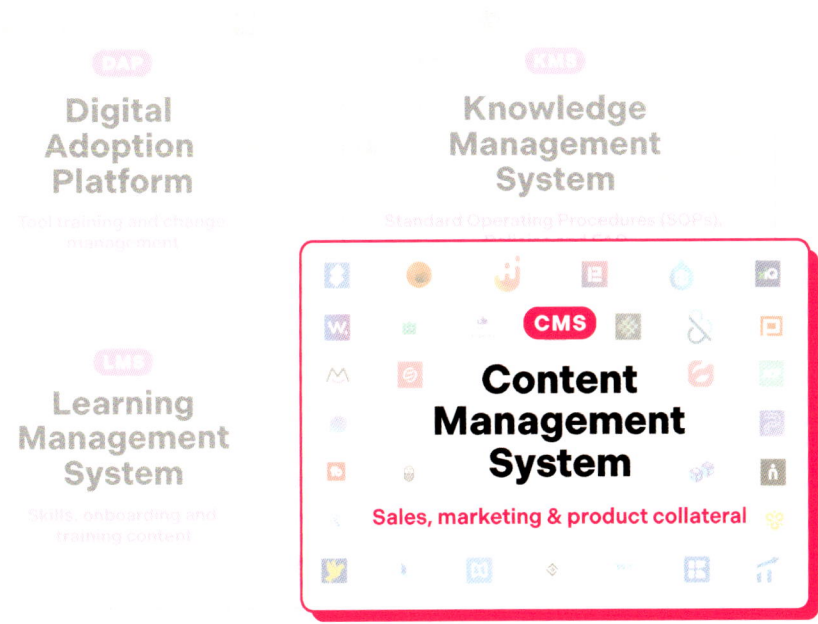

Content Management Systems

The need for a solution to host all types of content led me to explore CMSs, hoping they might offer an answer.

> **Content Management System (CMS)**
> *noun*
>
> A software application that lets users store, create, manage, share, and track usage of marketing and sales collateral.

Then, the messaging centered on solving content management challenges like tagging, organization, and content usage tracking; it was targeted toward Marketing. It's important to note that "CMS" also commonly refers to platforms like WordPress, which marketing teams use to manage website content.

Today, their messaging and capabilities focus more on addressing the enablement needs of sales reps, expanding the content they store to sales collateral.

Along with their ability to host various file formats, what separated a CMS from a KMS was the **emphasis on content engagement analytics**. I had zero visibility into what documentation or content our teams were using so that value proposition appealed to me.

But beyond tracking internal content usage, most CMS platforms offer unique tracking links that reps can send to customers to monitor how they interact with content. Was our marketing team wasting time creating content that no one bothered to use or share? Possibly.

And while valuable for our broader content strategy, buyer engagement tracking was a secondary concern compared with our broader enablement challenges like content discovery and decay.

Glorified filing cabinets, better aesthetics

Despite some of the potential perks of various CMS platforms, as I reviewed them, I felt like I was having déjà vu. Just as with many KMS platforms, I was disappointed by most options' user experiences. The interfaces were often clunky and outdated, reminiscent of software from a bygone era. Many content structures, still today, haven't evolved beyond digital recreations of file cabinets and drawers, clinging to familiar folders and labels instead of exploring new approaches.

To be honest, they didn't feel much different from our existing Google Drive setup, except for their browsable interfaces. They're another destination repository, albeit optimized with "intranet-like" features like home pages or custom pages, to visually display and organize content, hoping this helps reps find what they need.

I felt then, and still feel today, a significant disconnect between the design of CMS platforms and reps' actual needs. While occasional browsing happens by reps, it's not the norm. Reps prioritize speed and precision.

Knowing our reps, they would default to the search bar 99% of the time. In fact, ask any sales leader—their teams live in the search bar. Yet, CMS providers push these complex browsing interfaces with a slew of layout options and customizable buttons to make your pages look pretty.

Sure, there will be a rare time when a rep *chooses* to "browse" through all of their content, but should that event be what teams are optimizing for?

Every fancy feature and "pretty custom button" adds to the system's administrative burden. This diverts resources from critical tasks like content maintenance and combating content decay. Would the majority of reps choose a quick search with the precise answer they need over a beautifully designed page? Yes.

The UX should be about efficiency, not just aesthetics.

A critical realization

Ultimately, I concluded that CMS solutions relied on an outdated idea of how people find information. Content discovery and delivery were glaring issues—the features weren't designed for use in the flow of work. This presented a problem because, having recognized the value of contextual information thanks to my exploration of DAPs, **I now considered seamless access to knowledge and content a non-negotiable requirement.** It's no wonder that still today, 92.3% of enablement and marketing teams believe that less than 60% of their internal content is used by reps.[4]

Fast forward to today, many of these platforms have *slowly started* to emphasize the delivery and discovery of content, which is a great thing. This shift reflects a broader trend in the market, as organizations increasingly recognize the importance of integrating knowledge into the flow of work.

And while some CMS vendors tout CRM integrations, these often prove complex and challenging to maintain. They promise to display content based on opportunity criteria, but the reality is usually a mess of intricate tagging systems and configurations that require heavy implementation and maintenance. These integrations often suffer from the same challenges as DAP: Any changes to Salesforce will break the connection. For example, if you update your sales stages in your CRM, the integration to your tagging mechanism in your CMS will break.

---

[4] Spekit. Spekit and Sales Enablement Collective Impact of Enablement Report 2025. Available at: https://www.spekit.com/impact-of-enablement-report

After looking at multiple options, I once again faced a fragmented landscape. Why were CMSs and KMSs treated as separate entities? It seemed illogical and counterproductive for our employees and our efforts to create a unified knowledge ecosystem.

But even if I implemented a CMS and a KMS, I still lacked a crucial element: a way to organize and structure my content optimized for onboarding or even ongoing training. Neither category offered a way to organize content into a logical sequential learning path, relying instead on simple folders that lacked the necessary structure for effective onboarding and training.

PROS
- File hosting
- Content tracking & buyer engagement

CONS
- Destinations optimized for browsing
- Admin burden & customization

WHAT'S NEW
- Deal rooms
- LMS capabilities

This realization highlighted a critical gap in my search. I wanted a solution that could centralize and manage our diverse content *and* provide a framework for delivering it in a structured, learning-oriented format. This led me to explore Learning Management Systems (LMS), hoping they might offer the missing piece of the puzzle.

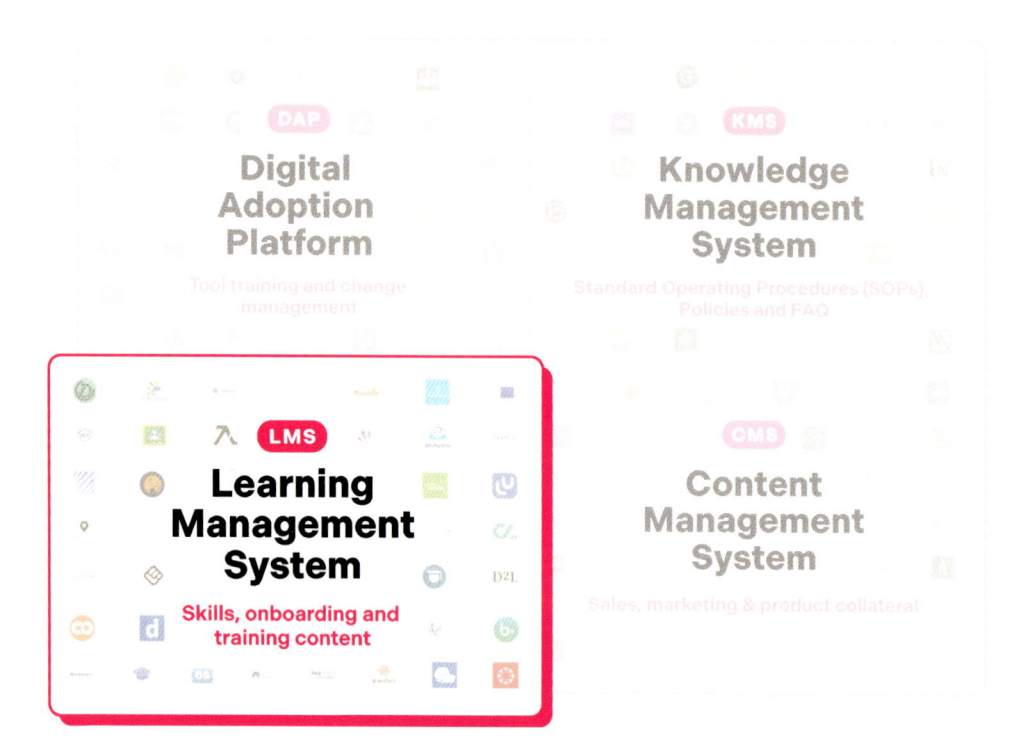

DAP
Digital Adoption Platform
Tool training and change management

KMS
Knowledge Management System
Standard Operating Procedures (SOPs), Policies and FAQ

LMS
Learning Management System
Skills, onboarding and training content

CMS
Content Management System
Sales, marketing & product collateral

Learning Management Systems

My search for the perfect enablement solution eventually led me to **Learning Management Systems (LMS)**.

Learning Management System (LMS) *noun*

A software application used for planning, delivering, and tracking training and educational programs.[5]

With hundreds of options available, I was initially optimistic that corporate LMS platforms would be significantly better than the ones I

---

5 SAP. What is a Learning Management System? Available at: https://www.sap.com/products/hcm/corporate-lms/what-is-lms.html

used both as a recitation leader and a student in college. However, as I explored deeper, I discovered that was far from the case.

The burden of course creation

The first issue was the sheer administrative burden of creating and maintaining courses. While designing full-fledged training programs initially appealed to me, I knew from my experience as a teacher's assistant in college how time consuming it could be. While the exact figure varies, estimates suggest it takes anywhere from seven to fifty hours to create just one hour of learning content!

While the concept of "microlearning"—delivering short, focused bursts of learning content—was gaining traction, it was clear that developing and configuring these courses would still be a significant undertaking. Besides, even if I had the time and resources to create them, maintaining them would be a nightmare, given how quickly our business was changing. The idea of an outdated course bothered me even more than an outdated document.

But even if I found an answer to the course creation burden, I still philosophically disagreed with "forcing" adults into training as the primary means of "enabling" them.

The "check the box" mentality

Forcing employees to complete courses and assessments felt counterproductive and reminiscent of my own experience cramming for my Series 7 and 63 financial exams.

Due to an admin error, I had just four days' notice. So, I did what I had mastered in college and crammed as much of the materials as I could over a long, intense weekend. Did I pass the exams? Luckily, yes. But did I remember the materials a few days later? Nope. I may have passed the exams, but the information evaporated from my memory shortly after. Ironically, it didn't matter since I moved into my business operations role before I could ever use them.

However, this "check the box" approach to learning, where completion is prioritized over comprehension and application, is a common pitfall in corporate training programs.

You know the drill: a new product launches, a course is assigned, followed by a relentless barrage of reminder emails and managerial nudges. It's a familiar rodeo that rarely leads to lasting knowledge or behavior change.

In fact, this is also why many organizations are shifting from traditional onboarding programs to a continuous "everboarding" model. Instead of a three-week information blitz, learning becomes an ongoing journey, reinforced over time.

That's why I believe that tracking completion is a misleading metric. It creates an illusion of learning without guaranteeing knowledge retention or on-the-job application. This often leads to a false sense of security and a failure to address true learning gaps within the organization.

Lack of personalization

To add to the above challenges, most LMS platforms fell into the trap of a one-size-fits-all approach. They delivered a standardized learning experience regardless of individual needs or experience levels. That's tolerable for the single HR or cybersecurity course employees are required to take, but not for an entire onboarding program. This was a major obstacle for us since we often hired reps with various levels of industry experience. A new hire with limited industry knowledge has vastly different learning needs than someone with years of experience.

Rep resistance

I wanted a solution that would excite our reps, not make them roll their eyes. Frankly, I cringed at the thought of telling them the answer to our chaotic situation was to take courses. That felt like adding friction, not removing it.

While practicing talk tracks for accurate call delivery is important, true retention comes from real-world repetition, coupled with ongoing coaching and feedback. To be clear, I recognize the value of structured learning in *specific* situations—for example, demo practice on a new product, where reps can record and receive feedback on their performance.

However, mandating courses or recorded role-plays felt like a Band-Aid, not a sustainable way to foster genuine, long-term learning and development. These specific use cases are the exception, not the rule.

Instead of imposing top-down learning initiatives, I wanted to create a system that empowered reps to take ownership of their learning journeys. A system that provided them with the knowledge and resources they needed, precisely when they needed them, in the context of their daily work. This approach, I believed, would not only be more effective but also more engaging and motivating for our team.

PROS
- Sequencing content (for onboarding)
- Knowledge checks

CONS
- Not effective for retention
- Heavy course creation burden

WHAT'S NEW
- Upload recorded demos and scorecards
- AI role-playing capabilities
- Partner portals

While LMS platforms offered some valuable features on the surface, such as allowing you to sequence information to form a course and tracking completion, their limitations were apparent. They weren't just inefficient; they actively worked against how our brains naturally learn and retain information.

Breaking down fragmentation

With every demo I endured, my perplexity grew. We needed a more agile, engaging, and user-centric approach to enablement.

The system was broken.

Despite the abundance of options, traditional enablement approaches consistently fell short. They promised vast libraries of information and streamlined learning, but the reality was a fragmented and frustrating experience for employees. How could a glorified digital filing cabinet or a library of online courses be the best answer to supporting reps in this ever-changing world?

What perplexed me most was the industry's acceptance of this fragmented approach. Many of these categories felt arbitrary, at best. In fact, Chapter Seven reveals a major ongoing transformation in the enablement landscape, including rebranding and consolidation.

The crux: the content engine

What did all of these platforms have in common? **Content**.

The crux of all of these platforms was a powerful **content engine** with core mechanisms around content curation, discovery, and insights.

I estimated that roughly 60% of their capabilities were similar, just repackaged under different names and user experiences.

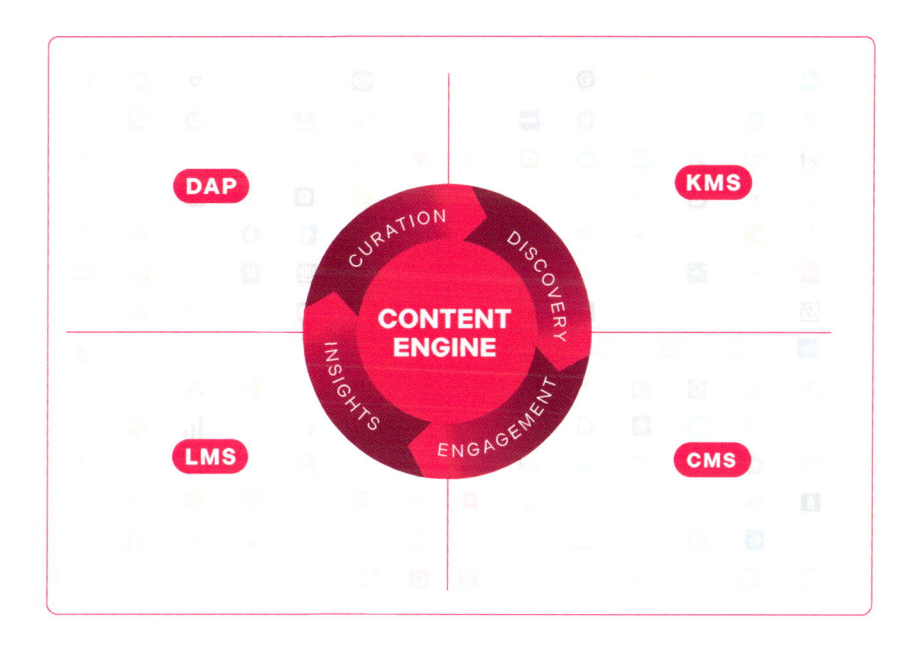

Those key capabilities included:

- **Content Curation:** content creation tools (editors, templates), content governance (version control, expiration dates, approval workflows), content import/export (sync, upload), organization tools (tags, folders), content metadata (custom fields, descriptions), content relationships (linking, hierarchies), and content lifecycle management (archiving, deletion).

- **Content Discovery:** roles, permissions, access controls (teams), search functionality (keyword search, filters, advanced search operators), content browsing (navigation menus, categories, recommendations), content previews (thumbnails, summaries).

- **Content Engagement:** content viewing (full-screen, embedded), content interactions (clicking, sharing, favoriting, marking read), content feedback (likes, commenting).

- **Content Insights:** content usage (views, downloads, shares), content interactions (clicks, shares, and more), content performance (knowledge retention, impact on business outcomes), content health (outdated or irrelevant content), and user feedback (content ratings etc.).

Differentiators: unique and valuable features

I believed that another 20% of each category's respective features offered unique, real value to solve the enablement challenge.

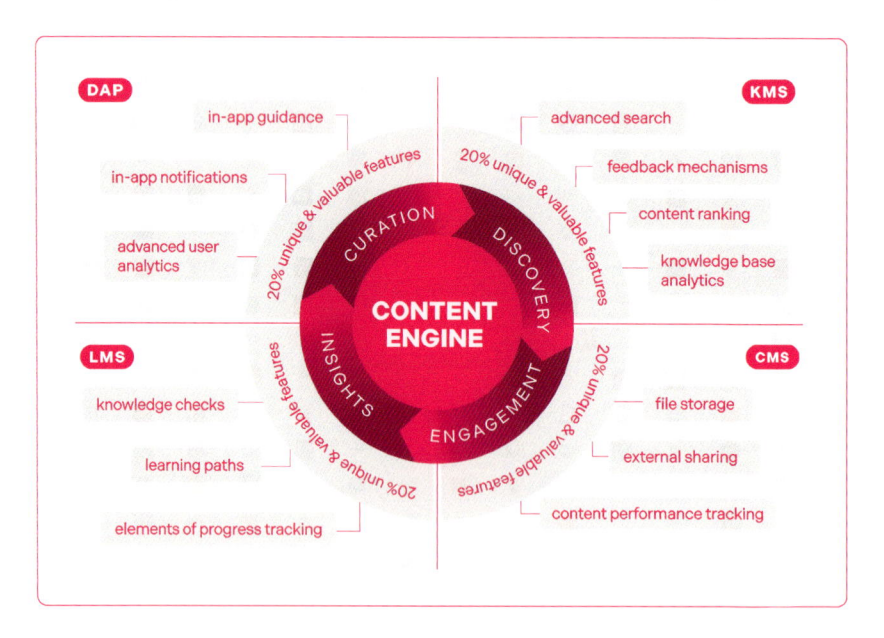

![Diagram showing Content Engine with four categories: DAP (in-app guidance, in-app notifications, advanced user analytics), KMS (advanced search, feedback mechanisms, content ranking, knowledge base analytics), CMS (file storage, external sharing, content performance tracking), and LMS (knowledge checks, learning paths, elements of progress tracking). Inner ring shows CURATION, DISCOVERY, ENGAGEMENT, INSIGHTS around Content Engine. Each quadrant labeled "20% unique & valuable features".]

The features within each category included:

- **DAP:** in-app guidance (walkthroughs, tooltips), in-app notifications (announcements, reminders, updates), and advanced user analytics.

- **KMS:** advanced search, feedback mechanisms (commenting, etc.), content ranking (relevance, popularity), and knowledge base analytics.

- **CMS:** file storage (cloud storage, versioning), external sharing (permissions, access controls), and content performance tracking.

- **LMS:** knowledge checks, learning paths (sequenced content), and some elements of progress tracking/gamification that are useful (many are not, in my opinion).

Bells and whistles: specialized features

The remaining 20% was a mix of flashy features that seemed more like marketing gimmicks than practical tools, along with specialized features that catered to specific needs and use cases that didn't apply to our needs.

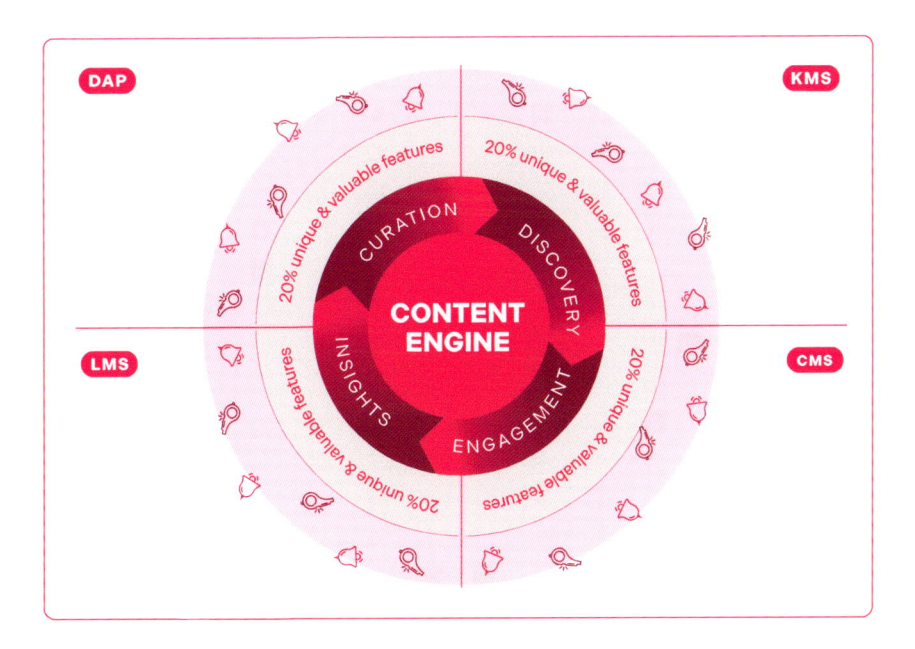

These platforms suffered from a severe case of "more is more." They boasted mountains of content and features so numerous they'd make a Swiss Army Knife blush (I'd know, I'm Swiss). I also knew that all of these "nice-to-have" features would also create a massive administrative burden. And honestly, after months of mastering the intricacies and administrating our Salesforce platform, the thought of navigating another complex system (or several) filled with endless customization options was overwhelming.

To be fair, some of these features demoed incredibly well. And today, with AI, they demo even better. It's easy to get momentarily distracted by all the problems we could solve, especially if the sales rep pairs the features with a compelling customer story.

But as I searched for a solution, I reminded myself that these bells and whistles reeked of low adoption rates and were distracting me from the core issues.

I recognize that some of these specialized features can be compelling for certain organizations with very specific use cases. For example, a large financial services company with complex compliance requirements might find tremendous value in super advanced LMS certifications. Or a global organization with a vast network of partners might rely on partner portals to streamline training and communication.

However, most companies run lean enablements that are always juggling dozens of priorities at once. They can barely keep up as their products and processes change, let alone think about implementing new, exciting features in their enablement platform.

The 2025 Impact of Enablement report conducted by the Sales Enablement Collective[6] shows that "not enough time" (38.7%) and "harder to implement than expected" (25.8%) were the top two reasons why certain enablement platform features weren't implemented.

Why don't enablement or marketing teams have time? Well, to put it in perspective, 48.4% of enablers spend 5 or more hours per week creating content and 64% of enablers spend 2 hours or more just administrating

---

[6] Spekit. Spekit and Sales Enablement Collective Impact of Enablement Report 2025. Available at: https://www.spekit.com/impact-of-enablement-report

the platform, with several noting more than 12 hours per week. Next, when you add the sheer volume of internal meetings we can't seem to escape and the constant context-switching that entails, that doesn't leave a lot of room to actually analyze what's working to inform your enablement strategy, let alone to "try" implementing new shiny features that are likely to overpromise and underdeliver.

Besides, the data also shows that the majority of these features aren't adopted, with features like presentation-building, AI-role playing and deal rooms being at the top of the list. In fact, 81% of enablers believe that less than 60% of their enablement platforms features are used. Which makes sense given the low content adoption rates we explored earlier.

If a rep can't find the resource they need in the first place, why would they be motivated to try other things in the platform? Besides, the more features you ask your teams to learn, the steeper the adoption mountain becomes to climb (which we'll discuss in Chapter Six).

It's easy to get caught up in the excitement of new technology and feel pressure to adopt every new feature. But it's crucial to prioritize the core functionalities that address your most pressing challenges. That way, you can avoid distractions that could negatively affect your overall enablement strategy.

> **PRO TIP**
>
> ## Avoid the "shiny-object" trap
>
> It's easy to get dazzled by flashy features and slick demos when evaluating software. To stay focused on your actual needs, create a simple evaluation grid before you embark on demos. Your grid should include:
>
> 1. **Top three problems**: Clearly define your biggest enablement challenges.
> 2. **Must-haves**: List the non-negotiable capabilities the software *must* have to address those problems.
> 3. **Nice-to-haves**: Identify any desirable features that would be beneficial but aren't essential.
> 4. **Top three evaluation criteria**: Determine your most important evaluation factors (e.g., ease of use, integrations, pricing, support).
>
> During your evaluation, have each person on your team rank the solution against this criteria on a scale of 1-5. The scores will help provide an objective view on effectiveness of each potential product.

Why fragmentation is detrimental

My evaluation of the landscape left me puzzled. Despite all the flashy extras, the solutions shared one thing in common: they failed to do the basics well. For example, they delivered:

- **A context-switching and content discovery nightmare.** The fragmentation would force reps to jump between platforms, searching for competitive collateral in one platform and internal policies in another. Not only would this be incredibly frustrating, but it would also be detrimental to their productivity and time spent selling.

- **Duplicate efforts and challenging content management.** Imagine needing to train your sales team on a new product launch. You create an LMS course with slides and quizzes. Then, you realize you also need a quick-reference playbook with key talking points, which you store in your CMS. And don't forget the battlecard summarizing competitor strengths and weaknesses in your KMS. Suddenly, you're creating the same information three times over, in three different formats, for three different purposes. I'm exhausted just typing that.

- **Persistent content decay.** Even if you managed to overcome the hurdles of clunky interfaces and feature overload, a more insidious threat lurked below the surface. Products change, processes are updated, and best practices shift. This constant evolution of information means that content decay is a real challenge for organizations. How do you ensure that your enablement content remains accurate, relevant, and aligned with the latest information? None of these platforms convinced me that they would solve the content decay problem.

In addition, the people, time, and resources required to implement, train, and maintain these systems were hard to compute—and way beyond what we could afford.

Providing easy access to timely, accurate content should be the foundation of any enablement solution. Enablement should empower, not overwhelm.

Yet, when I went looking for a solution in 2017, the existing landscape seemed designed to do the opposite—and left me dreaming of something that didn't exist.

At least, not yet.

CHAPTER 3

The answer: Just-In-Time Enablement

HIGHLIGHTS ─────────────────────────

Witness the start of a new vision for enablement.

Learn about the journey from traditional training to a future where learning seamlessly integrates with the flow of work.

Discover how Just-In-Time Enablement offers a personalized, contextualized, and simple alternative to traditional enablement platforms.

Explore the future of content and the role AI can play in creating a unified, dynamic, and measurable enablement experience.

After evaluating the fragmented landscape, I concluded that the solutions available didn't provide what we needed. I craved a simple, unified platform that could cater to each rep's individual needs, delivering knowledge and resources within their CRM, email, or other tools.

This ideal platform would **combine the best of all the platforms** I'd evaluated, be **easy to use** for our reps, and be **easy to administer** for our small, nimble team, allowing us to keep pace with our ever-changing business needs.

I imagined a world in which:

- Employees have everything they need to excel at their fingertips, just in time.
- Learning naturally happens in the flow of work and is personalized for each employee.
- Change is easy to master.
- Content is accurate, updating automatically with your business, and decay is no longer a problem.
- Understanding what's working or what gaps exist from an enablement perspective is easy.

Accidentally, I started designing a solution. This became my vision for **Just-In-Time Enablement** and, ultimately, the start of my journey as an entrepreneur.

SALES EFFICIENCY ↑

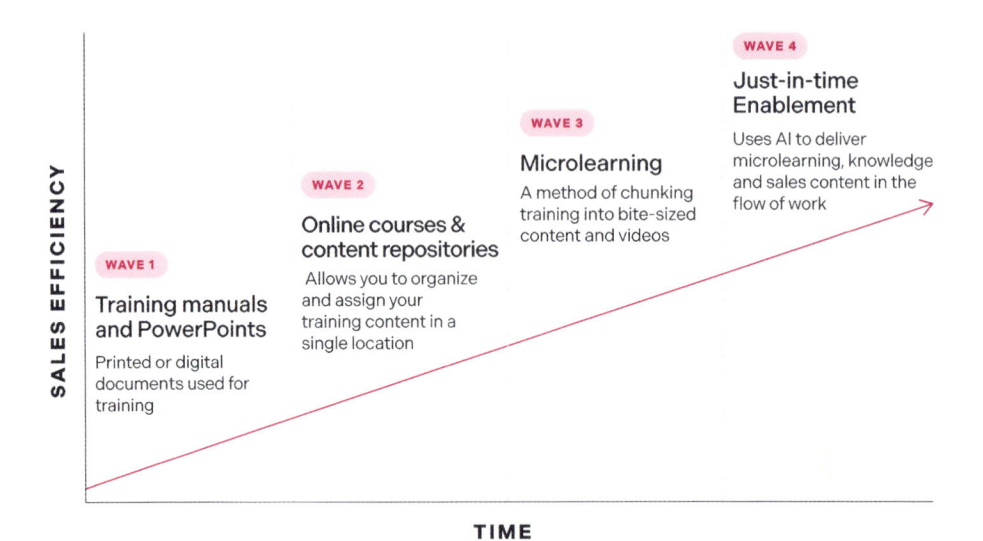

WAVE 1
Training manuals and PowerPoints
Printed or digital documents used for training

WAVE 2
Online courses & content repositories
Allows you to organize and assign your training content in a single location

WAVE 3
Microlearning
A method of chunking training into bite-sized content and videos

WAVE 4
Just-in-time Enablement
Uses AI to deliver microlearning, knowledge and sales content in the flow of work

TIME →

Just-In-Time Enablement: The next wave of learning technology

The evolution of workplace learning has been a steady march toward greater relevance and efficiency. From printed training manuals to LMS courses, each step builds upon the last. Microlearning emerged, offering bite-sized content ("chunking") for easier consumption. But something was still missing.

We needed a solution that would provide the correct information at the moment of need within the flow of work. The approach of just-in-time learning, inspired by pioneers in the field and echoing the efficiency principles of the Toyota production line, was gaining traction. Yet, my search hadn't led me to any technology solution truly embodying it. The closest was DAPs, but they were still far from ideal.

That's why we created Spekit.

While Just-In-Time Enablement shares the "right-information-at-the-right-time" principle with just-in-time learning, it transcends the limitations of purely learning-focused content. Instead, it encompasses all the resources an employee needs to succeed—from knowledge bases and training modules to the sales collateral they need to close deals and real-time coaching. This holistic approach empowers employees to perform their best at every moment, driving continuous improvement, adapting to changing needs, and positively impacting revenue.

For reps: a personalized enablement assistant

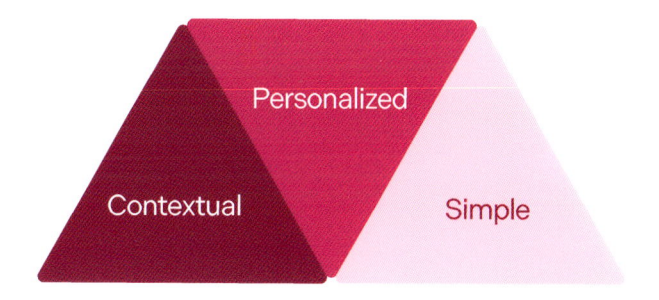

For reps, Just-In-Time-Enablement means having a personalized enablement assistant at every step in their workflow, providing coaching, generating answers, or recommending content. It's enablement that is:

- **Contextual**: enabled in the Flow of Work™.

- **Personalized**: tailored to each rep's precise needs.

- **Simple**: effortless and intuitive to use and take action.

Harnessing the power of AI, Just-In-Time Enablement personalizes the enablement experience. It empowers reps to succeed by anticipating their needs and delivering targeted support in the perfect format at the ideal moment—all within a streamlined and intuitive experience that feels like a natural extension of their workflow.

It's like having a personal enablement concierge whispering the exact information a rep requires in the heat of the moment.

Importantly, Just-In-Time Enablement is also rooted in the power of context and the science of how we learn (which we'll explore in the next chapter). It addresses the two most glaring issues I encountered in traditional enablement solutions:

- **Fragmentation and context switching**: no more jumping between multiple systems, disrupting workflow, and hindering productivity.
- **Lack of relevance and timeliness**: instead, information is delivered on time and in context, leading to better retention and maximized opportunities.

Reimagining content: unified, dynamic, measurable

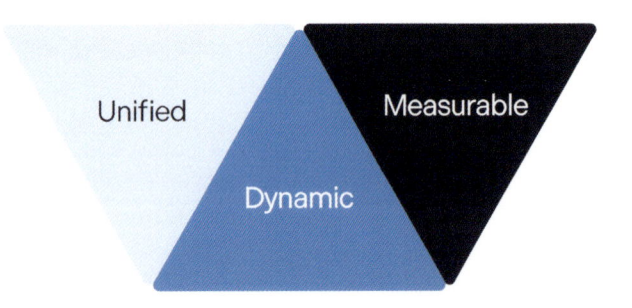

Delivering on this vision meant overcoming fragmentation and content decay.

To achieve this, we would need to innovate on the crux of the problem: the content engine. We envisioned a platform that was:

- **Unified**: one platform with modular and connected content.
- **Dynamic**: intelligent content curation that prevents decay.

- **Measurable**: provides valuable insights that have a real business impact.

Building a unified platform required a foundation of unparalleled flexibility and a modular approach to content. The solution needed to support any content format and type, ensuring seamless syncing to existing content solutions. This flexible core, paired with an equally adaptable UX, would allow content to be repurposed for various use cases across the employee journey.

The platform would also need to automate the tedious parts of content curation. For fast-moving organizations, automated content delivery and decay-prevention mechanisms, without cumbersome integrations and overhead, are no longer a luxury—they're a necessity.

The idea for Spekit was born

The name was one of the first things I came up with. It was a deliberate play on the word "spec," short for specification—those detailed descriptions of how things should be done. My vision was for a "Spek" to become an integral part of our everyday language, seamlessly woven into our communication and operations.

Imagine it: "Did you check the Spek for that?" or "Just Spek it!" Like "Googling" something or "Zooming" into a meeting, "Speking" would become synonymous with finding the information you need right when you need it.

And that "K"? It's a subtle nod to both "Knowledge" and "Kit" because Spekit is more than just a knowledge base; it's a comprehensive toolkit designed to empower teams with the knowledge they need to excel.

Before I knew it, I had a bug I couldn't shake. I was still at RealtyShares and had just received a huge promotion to chief of staff to our new incoming CEO, but building Spekit was all I thought about. "If only we had Spekit" became a constant refrain in my head. The idea wouldn't go away. Every meeting and every obstacle became a glaring reminder of how much we needed **Spekit**.

I didn't come from a family of entrepreneurs, nor did I set out to start a company in my 20s. I knew nothing about the fundraising process and had more questions than answers. (The truth is: I still do).

> "If it was easy, it would have already been done."

But I knew there had to be a better way. My conviction became an obsession strong enough to overcome every other feeling of doubt and fear.

It was a bold vision I knew would be hard to accomplish. Because as my co-founder, Zari, has always said, "If it was easy, it would have already been done."

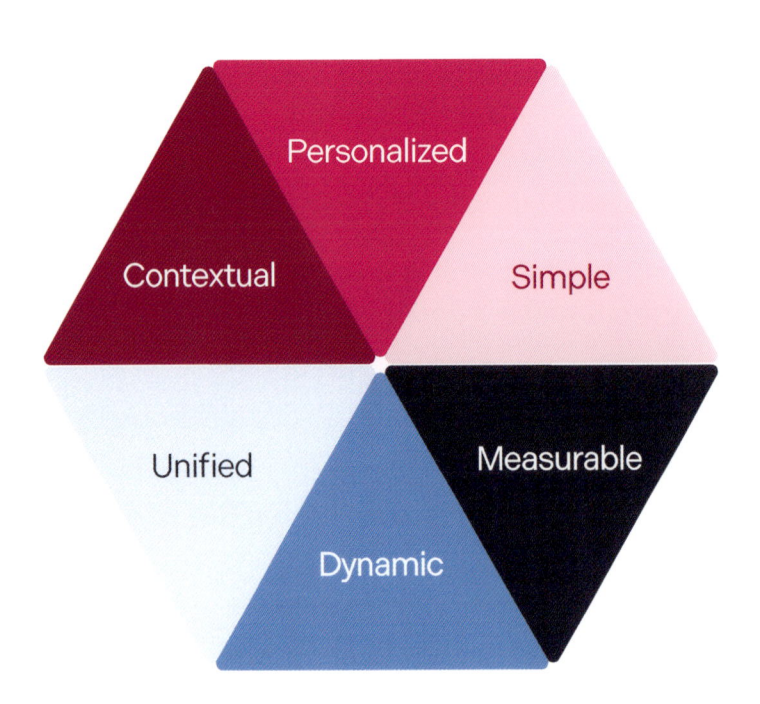

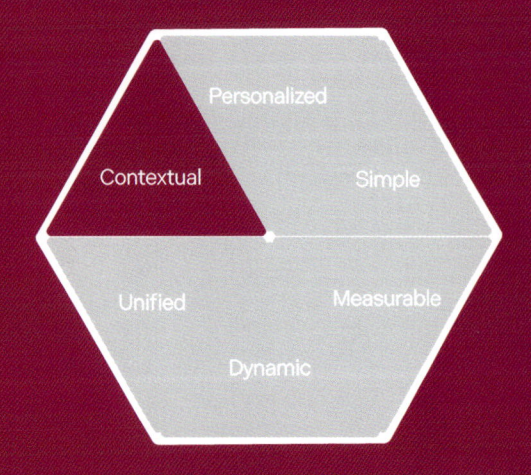

CHAPTER 4

Just-In-Time Enablement is contextual

HIGHLIGHTS

Learn about our goldfish memory, why we forget, and the negative effect of context-switching and cognitive load on memory function.

Discover the science behind how Just-In-Time Enablement combats our natural tendency to forget by delivering information precisely when it's needed.

Explore the benefits of contextual learning and why it leads to better comprehension, improved recall, and the increased application of knowledge.

Uncover how AI supercharges contextual learning with a just-in-time approach, unlocking a world of enablement possibilities.

In February 2018—just four months after I first pitched the idea to Zari—I left RealtyShares to pursue building Spekit with her. I wanted to transform enablement not just for one company but for every organization. The question, however, was whether Just-In-Time Enablement would work to solve our problems.

To answer that, we needed to go beyond surface-level assumptions and understand why enablement didn't work for reps. For us, that started with getting clear on a crucial question: **how do reps *actually* learn and retain information**?

Understanding how we learn as humans is essential for harnessing the power of technology to solve the persistent problem of knowledge retention. And that research would be crucial in our vision of building a solution that reps would use and love.

So, we turned to data and science. While I'm not a scientist, I've always been fascinated by how things work. As a teenager, I was captivated by physics—the magic of light, electricity, and the universe's intricate design. Today, my curiosity centers on the human mind. I love spending time immersed in scientific journals, podcasts, and books, exploring the intricacies of our brains and how to unlock our potential. Ultimately, I believe that understanding how to optimize our brains for peak performance is the ultimate job security in an age of automation.

That's what this chapter is all about. It explores the fascinating world of cognitive science and reveals why context *is* king when it comes to effective enablement.

Contextual learning is a learning approach grounded in science.

> ## What is contextual learning?
>
> Contextual learning is a teaching or training approach that connects new information to real-life situations or experiences. Instead of learning in isolation, students understand concepts better because they can see how they apply to the world around them.

We'll uncover the limitations of traditional training and discover how understanding the intricacies of memory, the power of reinforcement, and the value of context can unlock a new era of workplace learning.

Goldfish memory: why we forget

Have you ever sat through a training session, diligently taking notes, only to find the information evaporates faster than a puddle on a hot summer day? This is our **"goldfish memory"** at work. Our brains, while amazing organs, are wired for efficiency, not static storage. They're primed to forget, especially if they're overloaded.

Unlike a computer hard drive, our brains aren't designed for passive storage. Information that isn't actively used fades away, following a well-documented trend known as the forgetting curve.

The forgetting curve

Developed by psychologist Hermann Ebbinghaus, this curve illustrates the dramatic decline in information retention over time without reinforcement.[7] In other words, you remember only 80% of what you heard after just one hour. After three days, you've forgotten even more.

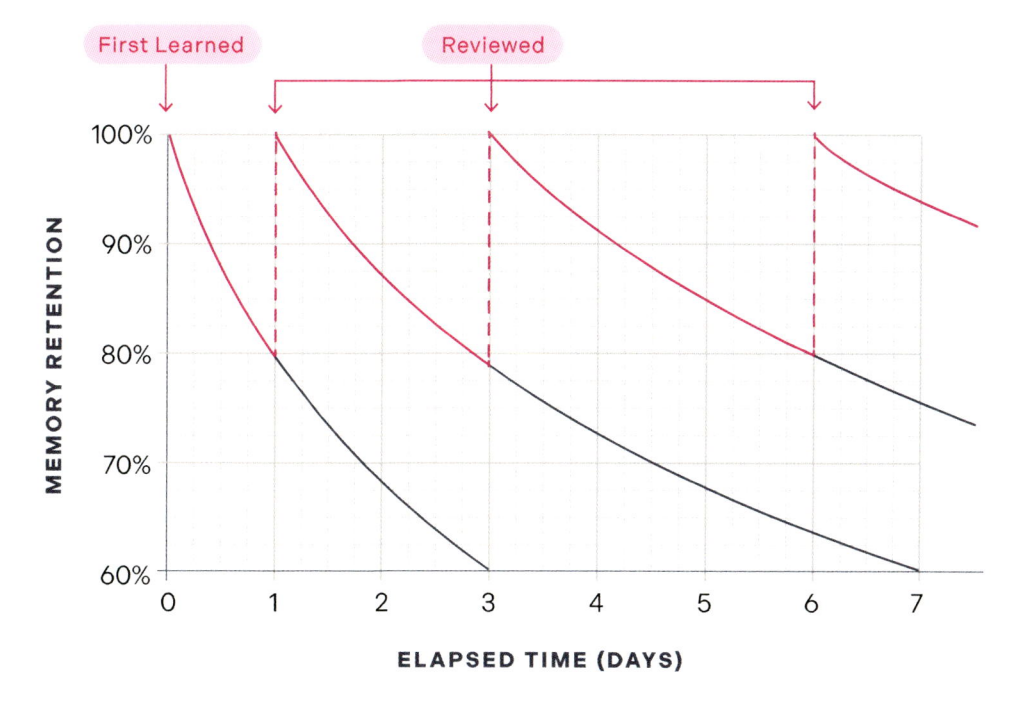

Traditional training methods like LMS courses—or even expensive events like your annual sales kickoff—often fall victim to this. They dump a large amount of information on learners only to have it vanish soon after because it's never reinforced or revisited.

Employees are expected to complete modules in advance, detached from real-world situations where they'll need to apply their learnings. Such training leads to information overload, low retention, and a disconnect from the immediate challenges that employees face. Why cram for a final exam when the real test is happening right now, in the trenches?

---

7 https://www.sciencedirect.com/topics/agricultural-and-biological-sciences/forgetting-curve

These traditional training modules rely on a "push" model, delivering information "just in case" the learner is ready or needs it at that moment, rather than "just-in-time" when they need it. And it doesn't work well. It's an ineffective approach to retention.

Why reinforcement matters for memory

The way information travels through our brains resembles a bustling metropolis. Information moves along neural pathways, like highways connecting different districts. These are essentially connections formed between neurons (brain cells) that allow them to communicate with each other.

The more a route is used, the wider and smoother it becomes, allowing information to travel faster and with greater ease. Just like revisiting a city landmark helps solidify its location in your memory, spaced repetition and reinforcement of information (also known as rehearsal) are required to strengthen neural pathways for long-term storage, combatting the forgetting curve.[8]

This is the essence of memory—the constant encoding, storing, and retrieving of knowledge.

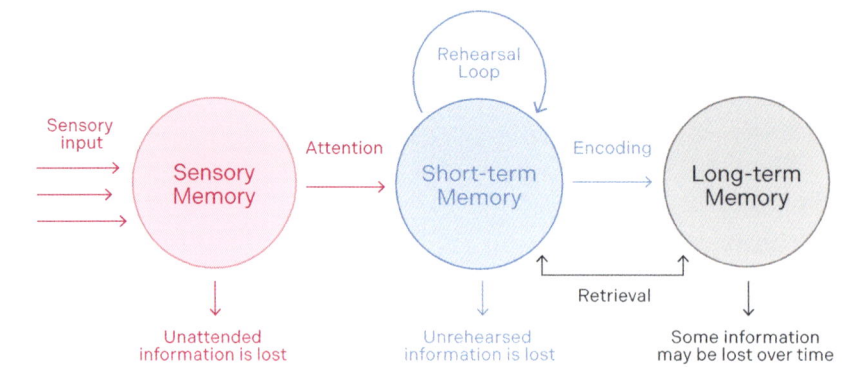

```
Sensory input → Sensory Memory → Attention → Short-term Memory → Encoding → Long-term Memory
                                              ↑ Rehearsal Loop ↓
                                                         ← Retrieval ←
```

Unattended information is lost | Unrehearsed information is lost | Some information may be lost over time

---

[8] Carr, Chris. Making It Memorable—Teaching Strategies to Support Recall and Retention. Stem Community Blog. 2021. Available at: https://community.stem.org.uk/blogs/chris-carr/2021/10/27/making-it-memorable-teaching-strategies

Cognitive overload: your memory thief

Learning starts with our sensory memory, which is what we see or hear. This is where attention truly matters because if you're not paying attention (e.g., distracted by your email during that virtual training), the new information might not make it past this stage.

If you are paying attention, the information moves to your working memory (also known as your short-term memory), where you actively process it. For the information to truly "stick," it needs to be encoded. This means it's transformed into a format your brain can store long-term.[9]

Factors such as attention, relevance, and emotional connection are all supercritical. This is why traditional training methods often fail, especially those that pull employees away from their work for lengthy sessions. When learners are distracted, disengaged, or feel the information isn't relevant to their immediate needs, their brains are less likely to encode the information effectively.

Cognitive load also significantly affects the memory's ability to successfully encode. To understand cognitive load, imagine your brain as a high-powered computer with a limited amount of processing power. With a low cognitive load, information processing runs smoothly, and memory is sharp. But as the load increases (thanks to multitasking and complex tasks), a person's mental central processing unit becomes overloaded. When overloaded, our brains struggle to focus and truly process new information.

An overwhelmed mind (experiencing cognitive overload) struggles to effectively encode new information. This leads to weak memories that are difficult to retrieve—like searching for a specific file on a cluttered desktop. The more information you have to sift through, the harder it is to find what you need.

---

[9] https://www.sciencedirect.com/topics/psychology/memory-encoding

Context switching: the productivity killer

In the modern workplace, cognitive overload is exacerbated by constant context switching. Even with the new AI features providing support, reps still spend 70% of their time on non-selling activities. In other words, they spend only 30% of their time selling.[10]

Most knowledge workers, especially sales reps, switch tabs hundreds of times per day. They're constantly bouncing between emails, CRMs, messaging apps, and knowledge bases. In addition, reps are bombarded with information, including industry updates, product changes, competitor analysis, and mountains of sales collateral. It's a relentless barrage that can leave even the most seasoned rep feeling overwhelmed and perpetually one step behind.

This mental juggling act makes it difficult to focus and process new

---

10 Salesforce. State of Sales Report. 2024. Available at: https://www.salesforce.com/resources/research-reports/state-of-sales/.

information. It also wreaks havoc on our working memory. Research shows that it can take up to 23 minutes to fully regain focus after a context switch.[11] These "switching penalties" increase throughout the day, leading to lost productivity and decreased cognitive capacity.

Sadly, much of the technology we've introduced to solve this problem has only made it worse. Just look at Chapter Two and the number of "enablement" technologies organizations use. Instead of streamlining workflows and empowering reps, many of these solutions add another layer of complexity and distraction.

> **PRO TIP**
>
> ### How to identify hidden productivity killers
>
> The fastest way to uncover hidden productivity killers? Dedicate time to shadowing your reps and conducting a simple time assessment. Here's how:
>
> 1. **Choose a task:** Select a common task like call preparation or follow-up.
>
> 2. **Observe and measure:** Shadow a different rep for one hour each week, tracking the number of clicks, tabs opened, and time spent on the task.
>
> 3. **Repeat and analyze:** Continue this process for a full quarter to identify trends and areas of productivity waste.
>
> Even with a limited data set, you'll gain valuable insights to inform your enablement strategy and collaborate with sales leadership and BizOps teams to optimize workflows.
>
> We'll explore the benefits of shadowing your reps in more detail in Chapter Ten.

---

11 Mark, Gloria; Gudith, Daniela; Klocke, Ulrich. The Cost of Interrupted Work: More Speed and Stress. University of California Irvine; Humboldt University. 2008. Available at: https://ics.uci.edu/~gmark/chi08-mark.pdf

Combatting goldfish memory: contextual learning

Reps need a UX that helps them, not hinders them. We wanted to eliminate context-switching and information overload. And we needed the experience to be seamless and intuitive, making it easy for reps to develop a new habit. That way, accessing and using the platform wouldn't be another chore; instead, it would become second nature.

The only way to achieve all this was to meet reps in their flow of work with the exact information they needed. In fact, contextual learning and delivery of information are the secret ingredients in combatting "goldfish memory" and driving knowledge retention.

The game of roulette that changed it all

I vividly remember the lightbulb moment that opened my eyes to the power of **contextual learning** years ago.

I was a business statistics recitation leader for a course at the University of Colorado, and I had just handed one of my students, let's call him Alex, a dismal performance on a probabilities quiz. His expression mirrored the dreaded "F" scrawled across his paper. Seeing his disappointment, I encouraged him to come to my office hours so that we could work on it together. To my surprise, he took me up on the offer and stopped by that afternoon.

We dove back into the quiz, but my attempts to rephrase the concepts with different terminology and examples felt like pushing a boulder uphill. Needing a strategy shift, I broke the tension with a casual question: "What did you get up to over the weekend?"

"Turned 21!" Alex proudly declared, "Celebrated with a little trip to Blackhawk, that casino up in the mountains."

A spark ignited in my mind. "Did you try your luck at roulette?" I inquired. His smile confirmed my hunch. "Perfect," I thought. "This could be the key."

Within minutes, the green felt of the roulette table became our classroom. Instead of abstract formulas, we translated the "chances" of winning into the very probability equations that had been plaguing him. The concept of odds wasn't just abstract numbers; it was the difference between red or black, a win or a loss. It clicked. That look of dawning comprehension and the "lightbulb" moment filled the room.

This experience with Alex wasn't just about teaching probability; it was a profound lesson in the power of context. By connecting the abstract concepts to his real-life experience with roulette, I was able to bridge the gap between theory and application. The "lightbulb moment" happened because the learning became relevant, engaging, and meaningful to him. The context also made it much more likely the information would stick.

For the following two years as a recitation leader, I changed the curriculum and started our probabilities class with a live digital game of roulette that the whole class played.

Not only was it fun, but the students reported that the concepts "clicked" more. I wish I had the data to prove it, but it would be interesting to see how the scores on those quizzes (which didn't change year over year) changed with this contextual approach.

> This revelation became the cornerstone of my belief that context has to be at the center of every learning experience we design.

This revelation became the cornerstone of my belief that context has to be at the center of every learning experience we design.

The benefits of contextual learning in the workplace

Just-In-Time Enablement, built on the foundation of contextual learning, delivers information within the flow of work. This approach offers numerous benefits, including:

- **Reduced context switching and decreased cognitive load.** By seamlessly integrating into employee workflows with extensions, Just-In-Time Enablement makes finding relevant information easy. No more hunting, and no more clicking marathons.

- **Increased information application.** By providing relevant learning prompts and resources precisely when and where they're needed, Just-In-Time Enablement ensures employees have the right context to apply information effectively.

- **Improved recall and comprehension.** Just as revisiting a familiar landmark can trigger a flood of memories, encountering information in a relevant context can improve recall and comprehension (this is called context-dependent memory[12]).

The data that supports Just-In-Time Enablement

On the surface, the value proposition of Just-In-Time Enablement seems obvious: give people the exact information they need, exactly when they need it. Now, there's research and data that support this intuition.

Gartner® research reveals that organizations that use just-in-time learning are:

- 2.5 times more likely to exceed seller revenue targets.

- 3.5 times more likely to exceed customer retention targets.

---

12 Heald JB, Lengyel M, Wolpert DM. Contextual inference in learning and memory. Trends Cogn Sci. 2023 Jan;27(1):43-64. doi: 10.1016/j.tics.2022.10.004. Epub 2022 Nov 24. Available at: https://pmc.ncbi.nlm.nih.gov/articles/PMC9789331/

- 2.3 times more likely to exceed retention targets than organizations that don't use just-in-time learning.

By delivering information in context, we can empower employees to perform at their best, drive better business outcomes, and create a more engaging and fulfilling learning experience.

> **PRO TIP**
>
> ### Add content shortcuts in your tools
>
> Don't have a Just-In-Time Enablement platform? No problem. You can still creatively embed content in the tools reps use every day.
>
> For example, you can leverage your CRM's customization features to:
>
> 1. Embed links to training resources within guided selling processes.
> 2. Add helpful definitions and tips to field descriptions (these can even include links).
> 3. Create dedicated help sections with quick access to key information.
> 4. Use hyperlinked content as default values in locked fields.
>
> A slightly busier user interface is a small price to pay for empowering your reps with instant access to the knowledge they need, precisely when they need it.

From just-in-case to just-in-time

This belief in contextual learning has shaped Spekit's UX since day one. While other enablement platforms today are playing catch up by adding just-in-time language to their marketing website, we built Spekit from the ground up as a contextual-first learning experience.

In fact, our octopus mascot Speki perfectly embodies the concept of contextual learning and delivery. An octopus has a central brain with smaller brains in each arm. That's Spekit! A central knowledge base (Speki's brain) houses all your valuable enablement content—sales playbooks, product docs, competitive battlecards, the works. Its tentacles (plugins in apps such as Chrome, Outlook, or Slack) reach into the tools your sales team uses every day, delivering the right information at the right time.

But these plugins or extensions do more than just deliver information; they gather crucial context, too. Like sensory receptors, they detect signals from the environment, feeding information back to the central brain. This creates a dynamic feedback loop, allowing the content recommendation engine to understand the "who," "what," and "why" of each interaction.

This gathering of context unlocks a whole new world for enablement and enables more personalized content, which we'll cover in the next chapter.

Context is king, but AI crowned it

Until recently, personalized, contextual learning and content delivery was a mere aspiration. The best we could do was manually map fields between systems, a tedious and error-prone process, although one that's commonly accepted for mapping content by stage in traditional CMS platforms.

However, AI is unlocking a whole new world of possibilities. It has the power to analyze vast amounts of data, understand context in real time, and deliver personalized experiences that were previously impossible.

From personalized recommendations on our favorite streaming platforms to tailored ads that seem to read our minds, context is shaping our digital experiences. And the world of sales enablement is no exception. The reality of AI-powered sales enablement is here, and it's evolving at lightning speed.

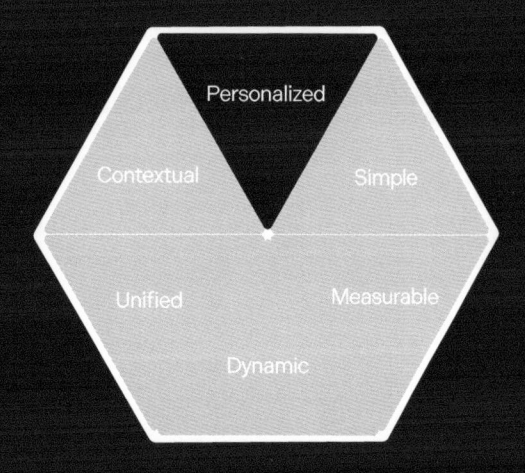

CHAPTER 5

Just-In-Time Enablement is personalized

HIGHLIGHTS

Explore how AI is revolutionizing enablement by delivering tailored experiences that drive engagement and performance.

Learn the basics of how AI and LLMs work to deliver personalized content recommendations and support in the flow of work.

Dive into the concept of AI-powered enablement assistants that anticipate needs, provide coaching, and deliver the right content at the right time.

Envision a future where AI personalizes every aspect of the employee journey, from onboarding and training to change management and continuous development.

AI, AI, AI

AI is everywhere. From your news feeds to company goal slides to new discretionary budgets, the new swanky " ✦ Beta AI" is showing up in all your favorite tools. Your marketing team is using AI for image generation and copy, your engineers are using it to review code, and job candidates are leveraging AI to help create their applications. Everyone is exploring the technology's potential. Eighty-one percent of sales teams report using AI today. Of those, 83% experienced revenue growth in the past year versus 66% of teams that weren't using AI. [13]

Many are questioning how to put AI to use. But an equally important question is whether AI is just the next hype cycle, following in the footsteps of Web3, NFTs, and blockchain—or is it a truly transformative force?

I believe it's a game-changer and we're barely beginning to scratch the surface of its potential to transform society and the workplace.

My appreciation for AI's potential began in 2018 at an AI conference in San Francisco. I was in the very early stages of building Spekit and looking to learn as much as I could. At the time, many of our ideas felt almost impossible.

Outside of feeling outnumbered as one of the few women at the conference, I was incredibly inspired from the moment the keynote started. Garry Kasparov, the chess grandmaster and former World Chess Champion, delivered an address about his historic match against Deep Blue, an IBM supercomputer.

---

[13] Salesforce. State of Sales. 2024. Available at: https://www.salesforce.com/resources/research-reports/state-of-sales/ © 2024 Salesforce, Inc. All rights reserved.

My mother taught me chess at a young age and even sent me to chess camp. I know the complexities of the game well. In his keynote, Kasparov shared how, in 1996, he lost a chess match to Deep Blue, marking a significant milestone in AI development.[14] For perspective, the computer was able to analyze 200 million chess positions per second. The match demonstrated the potential for computers to surpass human capabilities in complex tasks. "For the first time in the history of mankind, I saw something similar to an artificial intellect," Kasparov said.

What's remarkable is that it took IBM seven years to develop a machine "smart enough" to beat Kasparov after experiencing initial losses in 1989. Fast forward to today, and the progress that took IBM decades is now happening at lightning speed - just take a look at the news of DeepSeek that shook the AI world.

AI is transforming our daily lives and the workplace more quickly than we could have imagined and has solidified my belief in its power to transform enablement and content discovery to being **more personalized and proactive**—anticipating each and every rep's needs.

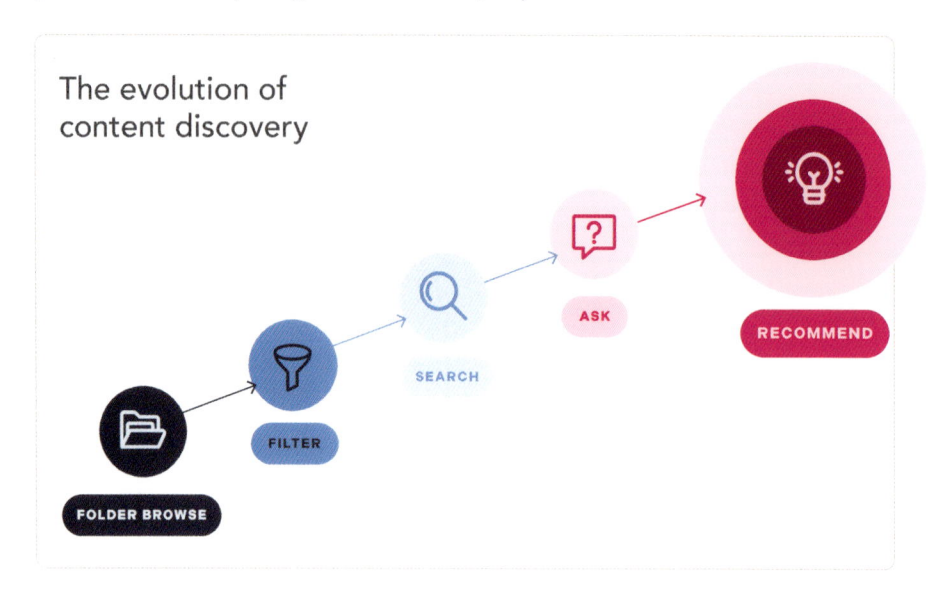

The evolution of content discovery

FOLDER BROWSE → FILTER → SEARCH → ASK → RECOMMEND

14 IBM. Deep Blue History. Available at: https://www.ibm.com/history/deep-blue

One-size (or case study!) doesn't fit all

In the age of AI, personalization is no longer a nice-to-have—it's a necessity. Yet, many organizations struggle to deliver truly personalized experiences, especially when it comes to sales enablement.

I witnessed the personalization challenge firsthand in 2021 within our own sales team when I was reviewing outbound messaging for our nonprofit sector.

Salesforce had just written an incredible case study[15] showcasing how the Southwest Airlines business team partnered with Spekit during COVID-19 to successfully transition to 100% remote and virtual training. The airline streamlined reps' access to training materials by embedding enablement in their tools. The results included significant time savings in content creation (60%) and change management communications (50%).

It was a huge success story! But there was a problem: Our reps started using this case study for *every* prospect, regardless of their industry or size, and it was the one attached to this very same outbound email cadence I was reviewing, which was designed for small to mid-sized nonprofits.

As a nonprofit with limited resources or a 300-person startup hustling to make things happen, does a case study about a 70,000-employee giant like Southwest Airlines even resonate? Probably not. It may even send the wrong message. A prospective buyer might think, "Whoa, this product is only for massive corporations with endless resources. We need something simpler that's built for scrappy teams like ours." The data shows this, too, considering that 86% of business buyers are more likely to buy when vendors understand their business and objectives.[16]

---

15 Salesforce. Solve It Stories. Available at: https://app.spekit.co/app/share/content/f4a7e176-fcab-4b5d-af50-e8f832011f92
16 Salesforce. State of Sales Report. 2024. Available at:
https://www.salesforce.com/resources/research-reports/state-of-sales © 2024 Salesforce, Inc. All rights reserved.

In an increasingly competitive environment, this lack of personalization might be the difference between a win and a loss

The irony, right? A tool designed to make enablement easier could seem intimidating due to an irrelevant case study.

What was more frustrating to me, though, was that we had the *perfect* case study to share with a nonprofit prospect: our excellent case study with the ALS (Amyotrophic Lateral Sclerosis) Association, the fantastic nonprofit working to find a cure for ALS and supporting those affected by it.[17] That case study highlighted how they leveraged our solution to successfully roll out Salesforce to 43 chapters and train their employees on new workflows.

The important question is **did our reps even know that case study existed in the first place or where to find it?**

Maybe the reps did know about it but forgot. Hey, it happens!

But maybe they didn't even know about it in the first place.

Either way, that's the gap that AI can bridge. Imagine your rep's super smart buddy (their AI-powered enablement assistant or copilot) is always there to whisper, "Psst, hey, use this case study instead!" This isn't just about finding any case study—it's about **recommending** the *perfect* one to resonate with each prospect.

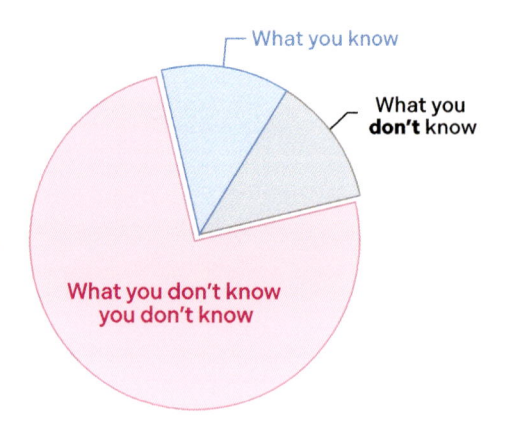

---

17   Spekit. ALS Case Study Video. Available at: https://app.spekit.co/app/share/content/4bbf6549-2797-4409-b9bf-f72f464d9b47

"You get a copilot! And YOU get a copilot!"

The concept of AI assistants, often referred to as "copilots" or "buddies," is rapidly taking center stage in the AI conversation. And now, AI agents are as well.

Just like Oprah showering her audience with cars, software companies are now handing out "copilots" like they're going out of style. Every major SaaS platform is developing its own version, each promising to automate tedious tasks that steal valuable selling time. You're already seeing Microsoft, ZoomInfo, and others battling for the same "copilot" title.

While AI assistants augment human capabilities, AI agents take it a step further, **autonomously** executing tasks and making decisions on our behalf. There's enough debate about the future of AI and whether AI agents will replace employees that I won't spend time on it in this book.

However, I do believe that reps will have personalized enablement assistants that proactively anticipate their needs to offer coaching and support as they navigate their workflows. This could involve drafting personalized email follow-ups with relevant case studies or surfacing competitive intel to help prepare for the latest competitive changes ahead of a crucial proposal call.

In fact, our first investor, Brett Queener, invested in Spekit in 2019 before AI and copilots were the buzzword du jour because he believed in the vision of "MySpekit," or what he called "your rep's personal buddy."

The future: AI-driven personalized content recommendations

How is this vision for a personalized enablement assistant possible? Well, AI can analyze your past behavior, current activity, and even your role to predict what you need or want next. In the realm of sales enablement, this translates to providing reps with the right knowledge at the right time and in the right way.

AI allows us to move beyond generic experiences and create personalized interactions. But AI needs fuel, and that fuel is data.

The good news is that businesses are sitting on treasure troves of data, a goldmine of insights garnered from every digital interaction. A lot of this data has remained largely untapped for years due to lack of resources to really process, analyze, extract insights or even use the data, like a powerful engine without a driver. But now, as we enter the age of AI, the game has changed.

AI can process millions of data points across a rep's tech stack, extracting key context in milliseconds. It can scan vast document libraries for relevant information and rank the results using intelligent algorithms, also within milliseconds. But these algorithms aren't just crunching numbers; they can understand and correlate success factors, enabling personalized recommendations for every rep.

If there's a single argument for CRM hygiene, this is it: clean data fuels powerful insights that ultimately drive better outcomes.

PRO TIP

Make data hygiene a priority

To motivate your team to maintain high-quality data, consider incorporating "data hygiene" or "pipeline hygiene" into their compensation plans. For example, allocate a small percentage of their variable compensation (e.g. 3%) to data accuracy and completeness. This encourages reps to prioritize data quality, which fuels more effective AI-powered personalization and better business insights.

Identifying needs: context signals

In the context (no pun intended) of Just-In-Time Enablement, to deliver personalized content recommendations, we need to understand what a rep is trying to achieve at any moment. This requires analyzing a variety of context signals and timing cues.

Think of context signals as clues hidden within a rep's workflow. These could be keywords or phrases in emails, call transcripts, or CRM fields that reveal their intent.

Here are a few examples:

Keyword Signal	Interpretation
"Pricing," "quote," "proposal"	Preparing for pricing discussion
"Competition," "alternatives," "compare"	Addressing competitor challenges
"Objection," "concern," "pushback"	Deal risks that need objection-handling
"Follow-up," "next steps," "summary"	Sending follow-up materials
"Case study," "testimonial," "success story"	Seeking customer proof points

The critical role of LLMs and RAG

AI, specifically natural language processing (NLP), large language models (LLMs), and retrieval augmented generation (RAG), can help decipher these clues. Consider the following:

- **NLP**: In simple terms, NLP empowers computers to comprehend, interpret, and respond to human language, much like a human would. Imagine NLP as a translator, breaking down human language into its components and analyzing them to extract meaning.

- **LLM**: An LLM is a generative model trained to write and think like a human.

- **RAG**: RAG is a technique that combines the strengths of information retrieval systems (i.e., like a search engine) with the generative capabilities of LLMs. Once the LLM understands the intent, RAG will retrieve the most relevant content from our knowledge base.

Gathering richer context

To provide even more personalized recommendations, the AI assistant can gather additional context across the rep's technology stack, including data about:

- **The rep**: their role, tenure, past performance, learning preferences, and content interaction history.

- **The task**: the specific task they're working on, their previous task, the tools they're using, and the desired outcome.

- **The customer**: the industry, the company size, and past interactions with the customer.

- **The deal**: the deal stage, the competitors at play, the decision-criteria, the use-case and more.

By combining context signals on the activities a rep performs with AI-powered analysis, we can create a personalized, activity-based enablement experience that anticipates needs and empowers reps to succeed.

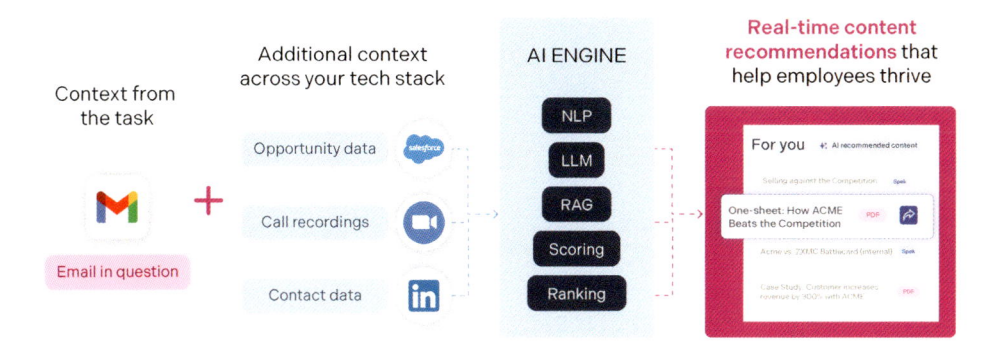

A real-world scenario

To illustrate activity-based enablement, let's imagine a rep who has a sales demo call. Here's how an AI-powered enablement assistant could help them craft the perfect follow-up email. First, the AI analyzes the call recording, identifying key topics, objections, and questions that the prospect raised. Next, it gathers data. The AI pulls relevant information about the customer and the user from the CRM, including:

1. **The rep's needs:** Does the rep need additional training to handle specific competitor tactics or customer concerns raised on the call?

2. **The buyer's journey:** What stage of the evaluation process is the buyer in? Does the prospect need a case study highlighting a similar switch from a competitor or perhaps a white paper addressing their industry challenges?

Now comes the magic. The enablement assistant is trained to analyze this context and extract the most important information to recommend the perfect content for the rep.

But the story doesn't end there. Now, AI can analyze the success of similar content used in past deals and identify what works best for your top performers. It can also factor in elements like content freshness, trustworthiness, and individual selling styles to recommend the most effective materials for every situation.

This dynamic combination of machine learning and generative AI creates a powerful feedback loop. The system constantly refines its recommendations based on real-time data and insights, ensuring your team can access the most relevant and impactful resources. It's like having a continuously improving knowledge base that adapts to your evolving needs and drives consistent sales success.

The outcome in this example might be as simple as recommending the perfect piece of content to the rep. Still, the personalized enablement assistant could also give them coaching on improving their email, offer an additional point to make based on the previous call, and recommend enablement for them to review ahead of the next call.

The power of personalization: a glimpse into the future

The call follow-up example is just a glimpse into the transformative power of AI for salespeople. We're on the cusp of a revolution in on-the-job learning and coaching, where AI empowers organizations to personalize enablement at an unprecedented level.

Personalization creates a more engaging, effective, and fulfilling learning experience, leading to better knowledge retention, improved performance, and, ultimately, greater success for both the individual and the organization.

Imagine a world where:

- **Change management is simplified**: Instead of bombarding your reps with newsletters, emails, Slack messages in five channels, and more, AI assistants unlock a new approach. The enablement assistant informs reps of process changes or new resources at the precise time (and location) they need to be made aware of that change — when they go to do that task for the first time, or that topic comes up for the first time. This targeted approach reduces distractions, removes friction, and promotes the immediate adoption of new processes and resources.

- **Your buyers are getting more personalized, tailored content**: The right content for the right title in the right industry at the right time. That leads to higher influence and a more substantial effect on sales cycles, win rates, and revenue.

- **Coaching and feedback are personalized**: AI provides real-time guidance, helping employees identify areas for improvement and track their progress. This feedback creates a dynamic learning environment where everyone feels supported and empowered to grow.

- **Onboarding is tailored**: New hires receive personalized learning journeys based on their roles, experience, and the types of leads they'll encounter. This ensures they ramp up quickly and contribute to the team from day one.

And finally, **everboarding becomes a reality.**

Evolving from one-and-done onboarding to everboarding

Relegating onboarding to a specific two- or three- week period and expecting reps to recall that information months later is a recipe for failure.

AI makes everboarding a reality, facilitating continuous development by recommending relevant content and training that's personalized to each rep based on individual performance, skill gaps, and evolving job requirements.

For example, imagine an onboarding experience where new reps aren't overwhelmed with the *entire* sales process at once. Instead, when they move a deal to the next stage for the first time, their AI enablement assistant steps in, providing just-in-time coaching and guidance. This ensures they understand the specific steps required to navigate that stage successfully and move the deal forward.

PRO TIP

Start shifting to an everboarding model

There are steps you can take now to move to an everboarding model that allows reps to tap into information as they need it throughout their learning journey.

- **Deconstruct your onboarding program.** What are the absolute essentials new hires need to know in their first week? Focus on foundational knowledge and skills, leaving more specialized information for later (i.e., high-level sales process success rather than stage-specific guidance).

- **Break training materials into bite-sized modules.** Instead of a one-hour marathon session on competitors, create a series of shorter videos or articles focusing on individual competitors or key differentiators. This makes it easier for reps to revisit specific information when they need it.

- **Make information easy to access.** Consider a one-page document your new hires can favorite with a list of important links. Categorize these links by topic (e.g., product information, sales process, competitor insights) so that rather than trying to recall the information, your reps can find refreshers on product updates moments before a customer call.

This approach not only empowers your team today but also lays the groundwork for a future where AI seamlessly integrates into the flow of work, providing more personalized and intelligent support.

Does this personalized, just-in-time everboarding approach eliminate the need for courses or live training? Not entirely. There will always be a place for dedicated learning in a distraction-free environment, especially for critical topics like security and HR.

However, we're witnessing a shift. Learning is moving away from cumbersome platforms and lengthy presentations towards a just-in-time model driven by the need for speed, personalization, and efficiency. Think of it like the evolution of internal communication. Slack and Teams didn't replace email entirely, but they became the primary mode of communication. Similarly, while traditional learning approaches will still have their place, just-in-time everboarding will become increasingly central to how employees learn and grow.

This is the future—a continuous, adaptable, and empowering approach to learning.

And it's closer than you think, but personalization is just one piece of the puzzle.

To fully unlock the AI's potential and create an effective enablement experience, we need to embrace another crucial principle: simplicity.

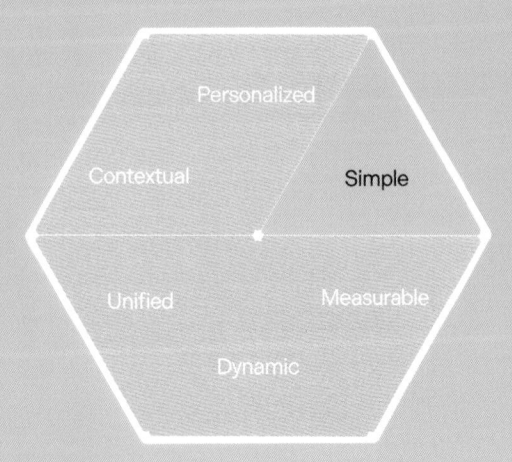

CHAPTER 6

Just-In-Time Enablement is **simple**

HIGHLIGHTS ────────────────────────────────

Learn how consumer apps have reshaped employee expectations and why your enablement platform needs to keep pace.

Discover why user experience and user interface design is paramount in the age of AI and the design principles to keep in mind. Uncover the psychology behind habit formation and how to design enablement experiences that encourage positive behaviors and adoption.

Explore the rise of conversational interfaces and envision a world where your enablement platform adapts to your every need.

Why are Facebook, Tesla, and Apple some of the most valuable companies of our generation? Yes, they're incredibly innovative. But also, they've prioritized their design to delight customers.

I believe that simple, beautiful user experiences will be the greatest differentiator in the battle for the rep's attention.

"Simple can be harder than complex: You have to work hard to get your thinking clean to make it simple. But it's worth it in the end because once you get there, you can move mountains." —Steve Jobs, Former CEO of Apple

This quote from Steve Jobs encapsulates the challenge and the reward of designing simple user experiences. In the realm of enablement, simplicity is paramount.

Many enablement platforms gather dust because reps find them more frustrating than helpful. It's an oxymoron—a platform designed to "enable" that hinders and frustrates. In this chapter, we'll explore why designing a rep-centric experience is critical to adoption.

Simple, yet *Spektacular*

When we began designing initial mockups for a Just-In-Time Enablement experience, one thing was clear: The UX and the UI design had to be simple. We didn't want to design a product that would end up as another tombstone in the graveyard of unused sales tools.

That's why Spekit's north star is *Simple*, yet *Spektacular*.

- **Simple** because in a world brimming with information overload and complexity, there's a quiet beauty in simplicity.

- **Spektacular** because, just like a well-crafted tool feels like an extension of the hand, Just-In-Time Enablement delights with every interaction, empowering learners to excel with effortless ease.

But achieving a product that's Simple and Spektacular isn't actually simple. To drive adoption and create success for sales reps and companies, the UX needed to be grounded in two key principles:

- **The science of learning**: We needed to leverage cognitive psychology and learning science principles to create an experience that promotes knowledge retention and application.

- **Habit formation**: We needed to understand how habits are formed and design an experience that makes it easy for reps to develop new, positive habits around accessing and using the platform.

To achieve this, we drew inspiration from user experiences of apps and platforms that reps use in their daily lives. Our goal was to make our platform so seamless and intuitive that using it becomes second nature, a natural extension of their workflow.

We live in a just-in-time, consumer world

It's no secret that technology has revolutionized our personal lives. From Uber to Instacart to Amazon, everything is instant. We order groceries, book rides, and stream movies with unprecedented ease and speed.

But what's often overlooked is how dramatically these consumer experiences have reshaped our expectations in the workplace. We've become accustomed to a level of speed, personalization, and convenience that traditional enterprise software simply can't match.

Employees now expect a **consumer-grade user experience** with any technology they encounter on the job. They're used to instant gratification, intuitive interfaces, and personalized recommendations. Anything less feels outdated and frustrating.

> Employees now expect a **consumer-grade user experience** with any technology they encounter on the job.

This is especially true as the next generation—Gen Z—enters the workforce. These digital natives grew up with smartphones and thrive on seamless information retrieval. Scrolling through social media? Second nature. Navigating a favorite app? Child's play. For this generation, hard-to-use interfaces and cumbersome workflows are not inconveniences—they're deal-breakers. Companies clinging to outdated enablement strategies risk alienating these tech-savvy employees, hindering adoption, and ultimately, affecting their bottom line.

The reality is that we've somehow accepted that it's "okay" for technology to be less convenient and intuitive at work, especially in the realm of enablement platforms. Which seems kind of crazy when you think about it. We spend half our waking hours at our jobs, yet getting a whole meal ordered, prepared, and delivered to our office via DoorDash can take less time than getting an answer to a simple question. Why are we settling for this disconnect? Why are we accepting a lower standard for our work tools?

Just think of the iconic Nokia phone with the snake game. Remember how groundbreaking it felt at the time? That phone was first released in **1997**. Only ten years later, in 2007, Apple released the first iPhone, transforming our expectations forever. The idea of using that Nokia phone today feels almost impossible.

In contrast, PowerPoint—arguably the most popular workplace training software on the planet—was invented in **1987**. That's a full decade earlier than that Nokia phone! And while it has certainly evolved over the years with better features and cloud collaboration, the core experience remains mostly unchanged. Compared with the quantum leap from Nokia to the iPhone, PowerPoint's evolution seems glacial.

Given the difference between workplace technology and what's available to consumers, can we blame reps for not wanting to adopt outdated platforms?

Your reps aren't lazy

First, let's dispel the common stereotype: "Reps are lazy." My experience paints a different picture. Most reps I've encountered are driven and ambitious and thrive on the thrill of closing deals. They dedicate countless hours to honing their pitches, building relationships, and navigating complex sales cycles.

> Most reps I've encountered are driven and ambitious and thrive on the thrill of closing deals.

However, their focus is laser-sharp—they prioritize activities that directly contribute to winning deals. Anything perceived as an obstacle to selling (e.g., virtual trainings) wastes their precious time.

For example, envision you're a rep on the last day of the quarter, about to close a deal. Suddenly, a customer throws a curveball, a technical question you weren't expecting. You stop what you're doing. The clock is ticking, and you know exactly where to find the answer: in your content repository. But that's when the struggle begins.

Multiple clicks, confusing menu dropdowns, poor navigation, a baffling interface; every extra second spent wrestling with the platform is a friction point, a roadblock on the path to closing the deal. And then you discover you're in the wrong platform. The journey starts over, this time in Google Drive. And then again in Confluence.

The result? Most reps abandon ship after ten minutes of painful tab switching and endless clicking. Faced with a time crunch, they resort to outdated resources, bombard their colleagues or Slack channels with questions, or rely on their fuzzy memory. By doing so, they risk relying on inaccurate information and potentially damaging trust with the customer.

Remember that saying, "Time kills deals"? It also kills adoption.

When a rep needs an answer or resource, they simply can't waste time fumbling around looking for it. As we discussed earlier, more than 90% of enablement and marketing teams believe than less than 60% of their content is used on a monthly basis. That's a whole lot of wasted effort, especially considering how much time goes into creating this content in the first place. If your content isn't stupid easy to find, unfortunately the outlook isn't great for it.

Designing for adoption: creating lasting habits

All of this UI overwhelm adds to reps' cognitive load, which, as we previously discussed, threatens their ability to focus, think critically, and make smart decisions.

To combat this frustration and drive enablement platform adoption, we need to shift our focus. Instead of simply building features, we must design experiences that encourage and reinforce positive behaviors. This means understanding the psychology behind how habits are formed. Because when it comes to software, adoption, and habit formation are two sides of the same coin.

Instead of simply building features, we must design experiences that encourage and reinforce positive behaviors.

Inspired by Charles Duhigg's book, *The Power of Habit* (2012) I've come to view software adoption through the lens of a three-step loop:

- **Cue**: The trigger that initiates the habit. For a rep, this might be a customer asking a product question.

- **Routine**: The actions taken to complete the habit. In this case, it's how the rep finds the answer to the question.

- **Reward**: The positive reinforcement that strengthens the habit. Here, it's the satisfaction of providing a quick, accurate response to the customer.

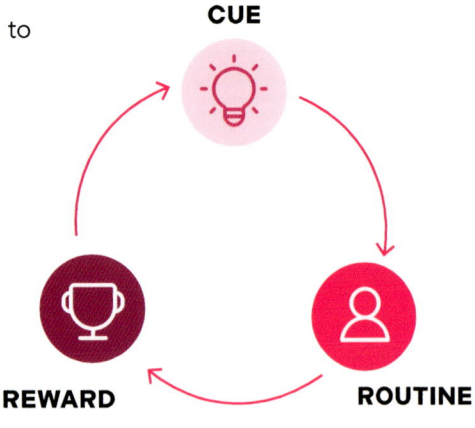

Any obstacle or difficulty in the "routine" makes it harder to complete the habit loop and less likely the rep will adopt the desired behavior. That's why minimizing "content discovery" friction—the time between the **rep's need for an answer (cue) and their ability to quickly give an accurate answer to their prospect (reward)**— is crucial for driving the adoption of any enablement technology.

We need to remove the unnecessary clicks, the extra buttons, the overloaded menu options, the confusing interfaces, and the lengthy searches and create a smooth, effortless path to knowledge.

That's why UX is so critical. A clean, intuitive interface, reminiscent of Apple's design philosophy, is essential. It should feel like a natural extension of their workflow, not "another tool" to learn and navigate. By leveraging familiar UX patterns and offering customization options to align with your brand, you can create an enablement experience that feels invisible yet is incredibly powerful.

The ideal experience is one where enablement feels completely natural, almost unconscious. It's an ever-present support system, always there to guide and inform, whether you realize it or not.

- **Conscious content discovery**: "I know I need something, and I'm going to look for it." This is the traditional knowledge-seeking model, with a user actively searching for information.

- **Unconscious content discovery**: "I don't know that I need something or that it exists, but it magically surfaces." This is the future of enablement, where AI anticipates needs and proactively delivers knowledge.

Most enablement platforms today are optimized for conscious discovery, but the future is unconscious discovery.

Designing for the just-in-time mindset

Over the years, I've developed a set of guiding principles that have shaped my philosophy around UX design, especially when building enablement solutions for busy sales professionals. These mantras apply to any enablement experience, whether it's a cutting-edge, just-in-time platform, an Intranet SharePoint site, or a simple Google Site. The principles of good design transcend technology; they're about creating an experience that is both effective and enjoyable for your users.

The key principles that are core to everything we design include:

- **Your reps don't care until they need to.** Reps are laser-focused on activities that directly contribute to closing deals. They don't care about a specific resource or skill until they're in a situation where it's critical. Then, they need that information delivered at the speed of thought; any delay can derail a deal.

- **One-click or bust.** Just as Amazon transformed the checkout experience with the one-click purchase, enablement should strive for one-click discovery, sharing, and action. Every click is a potential friction point. Searches with no results, searches without clicks, and searches requiring multiple clicks are the death of adoption.

- **Don't reinvent the wheel.** Avoid introducing new user experiences and patterns that reps need to learn. It only adds to their cognitive load, which is detrimental to adoption. Instead, mirror existing UX patterns, especially those of common consumer platforms. And make the UX as delightful as possible.

- **Less is more.** Every extra button, every extra tag, and every menu item should be scrutinized. Every extra element risks adding confusion and cognitive load—one more thing to remember.

- **Enablement is a means to an end.** Unlike platforms that benefit from "time spent," where engagement is the primary metric, Just-In-Time Enablement should prioritize efficiency and effectiveness. The goal is not to keep reps glued to the platform but to empower them to master or find the information they need quickly and get back to selling.

- **The delta is what matters.** When content is updated, reps need to know what's changed, not wade through the entire document again. Surfacing the delta—the specific changes since they last viewed the content—is crucial for efficient knowledge consumption and adoption.

Designing for a future of AI

Finally, as discussed in the previous chapter, AI is transforming the modern workplace, and user interface design is no exception.

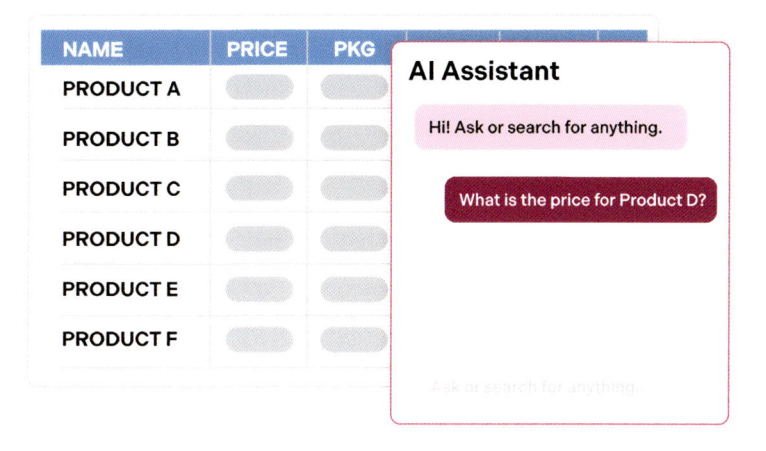

Inspired by OpenAI's ChatGPT interface, most rep technologies are moving away from traditional tables, forms, and list views—the Excel-inspired interfaces that dominated our early computer experiences.

Instead, they're favoring something altogether more human: conversation.

I believe that the future of most SaaS technology, especially revenue technology, rests in conversational interfaces where users can "ask" questions or query data in natural language and receive answers with human-like responses. A notable example is in conversation intelligence tools, where a rep can ask questions such as, "What were my buyer's top priorities on the call?" and get a natural response back.

Why is this evolution happening? Because it mirrors behaviors we already know from our consumer lives. Think of how we use Google or ChatGPT. We simply ask a question and receive an answer. This is the experience users now expect in the workplace.

PRO TIP

Train reps on how to get better answers from AI

More than one-third of teams list "insufficient employee training on how to use AI" as a top roadblock to AI adoption.[18]

While the rise of conversational interfaces is exciting, the quality of answers depends on the framing of the question and the quality of the underlying content (as we'll discuss in the upcoming chapters). Just like a search engine, AI needs clear, specific prompts to deliver accurate and helpful responses.

To empower your reps to become AI masters, consider these strategies:

1. **Identify "key steps" that will benefit from AI**: Look for points in your reps' workflows where they're most likely to need

---

[18] Salesforce. State of Sales. 2024. Available at: https://www.salesforce.com/resources/research-reports/state-of-sales/ © 2024 Salesforce, Inc. All rights reserved.

information or ask questions (e.g., account research, process navigation, proposal creation).

2. **Prompt engineering 101**: Provide quick, bite-sized training on how to craft effective prompts for AI, including tips on phrasing, keywords, and specifying the desired output.

3. **Encourage practice by making It fun**: Host a "best prompt for X" competition with a fun prize to encourage reps to practice and master the art of prompt engineering. The competition can be done in a virtual group workshop, incorporated into a Sales Kickoff, or asynchronously using internal Teams or Slack channels. This will encourage your team to get familiar with the small nuances and the specificity required to generate better answers.

4. **Build a prompt library**: Create a readily accessible library of pre-written prompts that reps can easily modify and use. This could be a simple Google Doc or a Topic of Speks that your reps can easily retrieve and copy/paste/edit into their various chat interfaces for best results.

5. **Promote ongoing adoption**: Create a dedicated channel in Teams or Slack where your team can share interesting AI use cases, tips, and success stories. To further encourage adoption, consider incorporating a short "AI Show-and-Tell" segment into your weekly sales meetings or all-hands. This provides a platform for reps to showcase how they're using AI, fosters a culture of learning and innovation, and reinforces your commitment to becoming an AI-first organization.

By investing in AI training and providing the right resources, you can equip your reps to leverage AI effectively, unlock its full potential, and drive better outcomes.

Imagine a UI that adapts to you

While the rise of conversational interfaces is exciting, there's a crucial caveat: just as reps despise juggling multiple apps and knowledge systems, they won't tolerate multiple AI assistants.

To simplify the UX, reps need a single, powerful AI enablement assistant that can handle the full spectrum of enablement needs. This means consolidating those "four different systems" and their corresponding assistants into one comprehensive solution.

> To simplify the user experience, reps need a single, powerful AI enablement assistant that can handle the full spectrum of enablement needs.

This all-encompassing AI assistant will become an indispensable partner, providing personalized guidance, anticipating needs, and empowering reps to perform at their best. It's a future where technology fades into the background, enabling seamless productivity and unlocking human potential.

This requires a UX that is fluid and adaptable. Imagine a UI that adapts to you, just like a chameleon blends into its surroundings. This is the future of personalized enablement, where the user interface seamlessly morphs to meet your specific needs at any given moment:

- **Need to get information on a competitor quickly?**
  The UI transforms into a chatbot-like interface, providing instant information.

- **Want to brush up on your negotiation skills before a key call?**
  The UI shifts into Learning Mode, creating a focused, guided

journey that helps you absorb information and master the steps individually.

This is the power of AI-driven personalization, as explored in Chapter Six. It's a UX that molds not only to individual preferences but also to the specific context of the moment, ensuring you always have the optimal interface for the task.

The urgent need for content automation

Unfortunately, even with a perfect UI and the magic of AI, there's a critical piece of the puzzle we can't ignore: **content quality**.

What happens when the "right" information is, in fact, wrong?

To truly leverage the power of AI for enablement, we need to prioritize content quality, ensure data accuracy, and demand robust analytics. That's why the most significant potential of AI for enablement teams is in automating content curation and governance.

This brings us to the three rules that will shape the future of content management:

- **Unified**: one platform with modular and connected content.
- **Dynamic**: intelligent content curation that prevents decay.
- **Measurable**: valuable insights, real business impact.

In the upcoming chapters, we'll dive into each of these concepts and explore how they can revolutionize your enablement strategy.

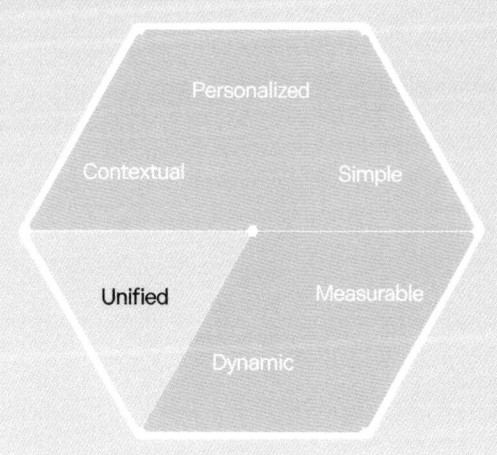

CHAPTER 7

The future of content is unified

HIGHLIGHTS ───────────────────────────────

Explore how the future of enablement hinges on a single powerful platform that breaks down information and technology silos.

Envision a flexible foundation that supports any content type, paired with an adaptable user experience that allows for effortless repurposing, adaptation, and personalization. Learn how a modular approach to content, inspired by software development and music playlists, can revolutionize knowledge sharing and drive agility.

Discover how a flat content architecture and AI can transform information from a static collection of documents into a living, connected ecosystem of knowledge.

"If I had asked people what they wanted, they would have said a faster horse." — Henry Ford, Founder of the Ford Motor Company

Henry Ford's famous quote rings truer than ever in today's competitive landscape. It's tempting to simply give customers what they think they want—a "better" CMS, an LMS with a few new features. I often tell our team that following that path would have been easier. Just look at the top CMS platforms; they're practically clones of one another, each frantically copying the latest features in a race to nowhere.

But here's the truth: After eight years and thousands of conversations with businesses of all sizes whose teams have tried countless enablement systems and endless tinkering, it's clear that no organization feels its enablement platform has truly helped them crack the code to effective, scalable enablement and content management.

Companies are stuck in a cycle of switching from one solution to the next hoping that one of them will magically solve their content adoption, decay, or syncing issues. They're waiting for that *one feature* in that other platform that will make all the difference.

Content management remains an unsexy, tangled, messy problem, and no amount of incremental improvement or "lipstick on a pig" will fix it.

I believed it eight years ago, and still today, the enablement landscape needs a complete rethink that addresses the two root issues:

- **Fragmented solutions:** Teams waste time and energy creating duplicate content across multiple platforms: a course in their LMS, a one-pager in their CMS, and a sales playbook in Google Drive, all for the same product launch. This leads to content chaos and makes managing the numerous assets challenging.

- **Complex hierarchies and rigid formats**: These systems, with their intricate webs of folders, subfolders, and tags, were built for a world of static, long-form content. Repurposing content, managing updates, and avoiding content decay have become herculean tasks.

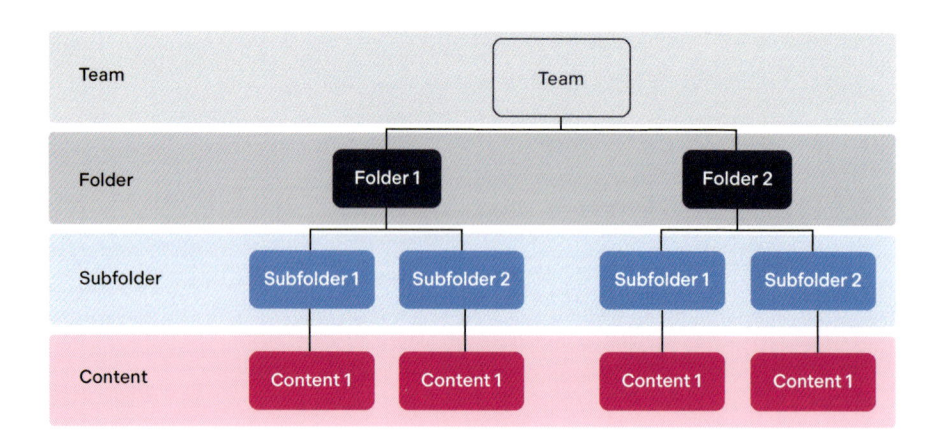

Team	Team
Folder	Folder 1, Folder 2
Subfolder	Subfolder 1, Subfolder 2, Subfolder 1, Subfolder 2
Content	Content 1, Content 1, Content 1, Content 1

Rethinking content: the key to unlocking enablement's future

Since 2018, I have believed that the future of enablement has hinged on a single powerful platform. This platform would break down silos, combine versatile capabilities with adaptable content to solve various needs and embrace the potential of AI. But the key to this transformation? Rethinking content itself.

We needed to radically innovate and focus our attention on the crux of building a scalable enablement platform: the **content engine**. That included the 60% of capabilities shared across platforms that centered around content curation, discovery, engagement and insights. The goal was to solve the persistent problem of information fragmentation and deliver knowledge seamlessly to employees.

> We needed to radically innovate and focus our attention on the crux of building a scalable enablement platform: the **content engine**.

But we didn't stop there. We also wanted to incorporate the best features (the "20% valuable features" we explored in chapter two) from other enablement solutions. Could we combine the strengths of Digital Adoption Platforms (DAPs), Knowledge Management Systems (KMSs), Content Management Systems (CMSs), and Learning Management Systems (LMSs) into a single, seamless experience?

We set out to build an enablement platform that offers:

- **The contextual guidance of a DAP**: providing interactive walkthroughs, tool tips, and in-app support, guiding users through complex processes and new tools.

- **The searchability of a KMS**: empowering users to quickly find the information they need with powerful search capabilities that span various content sources.

- **The content storage and analytics of a CMS**: enabling efficient

- content management, sharing, and usage tracking across diverse formats.

- **The structured learning of an LMS**: facilitating organized learning journeys and knowledge checks to support employee onboarding and development.

Finally, we decided to strategically ignore the "bells and whistles" (the remaining 20% of features) that these platforms offered. Instead, we doubled down on solving the core issues of content discovery and decay. Over time, we would evaluate whether any specialized features were truly essential for our customers.

A unified approach: beyond bolt-ons and feature wars

When I first started fundraising for Spekit in 2018 and 2019, many investors turned me down. They didn't believe that consolidating each of these categories' capabilities into one enablement solution was possible or necessary.

Fast-forward to today, and that consolidation is happening across the entire GTM tech stack. We're seeing massive convergence among customer engagement platforms, with conversation intelligence and forecasting all merging into single revenue platforms. Where companies once needed a half dozen different tools, soon they'll just want one.

The same trend is sweeping through the learning and content space. Platforms are merging, functionalities are converging, and the lines between categories are blurring. CMS platforms are rebranding themselves as "Enablement Platforms" acknowledging the growing need for solutions beyond basic content management.

They're also shifting their messaging and product strategy to appeal to their new primary target buyer: sales enablement.

This shift is evident in the recent scramble by CMS companies to acquire or build LMS or KMS solutions to stay competitive. For example, Showpad acquired LearnCore in 2018[19], then, Seismic acquired Lessonly in 2021[20]. Similarly, LMS platforms like Allego are building or acquiring CMS capabilities and CMS platforms like Highspot are building LMS capabilities.

> **An enablement solution that grew from other products is very different from one built with a unified content experience in mind.**

But there's a challenge with this approach to consolidation: Sure, you might have "CMS" and "LMS" capabilities under the same roof with a shared login, but often you're left with two completely different user experiences. The best you get today is perhaps a shortcut to a course when looking at a document.

A product that grew from other products is very different from one built with a unified experience in mind. This is especially true for enablement platforms. While the race to bolt on features and frantically make acquisitions to keep pace is ongoing, I've believed since day one in the need for a fundamentally different approach—a unified content experience.

This means resisting the temptation to simply slap together disparate functionalities or chase the latest "feature war" trends. Instead, it requires a focus on creating a truly integrated platform—a single source of truth with a seamless experience for both content creators and consumers. This vision requires reimagining the very structure of content itself, not just applying a fresh coat of paint.

---

19 Showpad. Showpad Acquires LearnCore to Deliver the Industry's First Integrated Sales Enablement Platform. 2018. Available at: https://www.showpad.com/press/showpad-acquires-learncore-to-deliver-the-industrys-first-integrated-sales-enablement-platform
20 Seismic. Seismic Acquires Lessonly. 2021. Available at: https://seismic.com/newsroom/seismic-acquires-lessonly-series-g/

Building a flexible foundation for a unified experience

I knew that building individual features like content tracking or in-app alerts would be the easier part. The hard part would be to get our foundation right: the content engine.

To build a truly unified platform, we first needed to construct a foundation of unparalleled flexibility—one capable of supporting any content format and type from any source (e.g., a customer's Google Drive or SharePoint). Pairing this flexible core with an equally adaptable UX allows content to be repurposed and adapted to solve different challenges across the entire employee journey.

A page from software development

"The smaller you make things, the easier they are to maintain."

This principle, embraced by software developers worldwide, is key to combating technical debt, which is the accumulation of outdated code and design flaws that hinder progress and innovation. Think of technical debt as the software equivalent of content decay in enablement.

Software development has embraced practices like modularity, composability, and Agile methodologies to tackle this challenge. By breaking down complex systems into smaller, manageable units, developers can confidently isolate issues, make changes, and adapt quickly to evolving needs.

The same logic applies to enablement content. The smaller the unit, the easier it is to maintain, update, and adapt.

By taking inspiration from these proven concepts, we can deliver a content experience as dynamic and agile as the businesses it serves, minimizing content debt and maximizing the impact of knowledge sharing.

Envision a content experience that features:

- **Bite-sized, modular content:** Information is broken down into small, reusable units that can be assembled and reassembled in various ways to meet different needs.

- **Connected content and concepts**: Clicking on a piece of content or a term in a document surfaces its definition, related resources, and other relevant information, ensuring consistency and accuracy across all materials.

This would allow your company's knowledge to flow effortlessly, connecting concepts and resources in an intuitive and interactive way.

Goodbye, monolithic content

Long, rigid content is in direct conflict with the vision of Just-In-Time Enablement.

Just-In-Time Enablement is about delivering the precise information you need, exactly when and where you need it. It's not about pointing you to a massive document and assuming you'll find the answer or forcing you to fast-forward through a lengthy training video. Instead, it's about providing bite-sized, targeted information seamlessly integrated into your workflow, empowering you to learn and adapt quickly without disrupting your productivity.

Consider the typical enablement content in most organizations today: lengthy documents, sales playbooks, and training manuals. These monolithic blocks of information are a pain to navigate, and they're even harder to update.

Want to make sure everyone sees that crucial update you made on page

> **These monolithic blocks of information are a pain to navigate, and they're even harder to update.**

15 of your sales playbook? Good luck with that. Your best bet is to tag your team in the section of the document and hope they actually read it, or blast out the entire document again and pray for the best.

The long-form nature of content quickly leads to decay (which we'll explore in the next chapter) and content duplication, particularly for processes.

Let's take a sales playbook as an example. Ideally, your sales playbook is the "bible" of your sales team, including everything from your sales process to your personas to discovery questions. We've had customers share their playbooks, and they're 120+ pages of content.

They're comprehensive, but there's also a lot of repetition. Some processes might be 80% the same for all teams, but the 20% that's different is what's important. For example, if you have a small and medium-sized business (SMB) and an enterprise sales team for your product, the high-level stages of the sales process are likely the same. But, the exit criteria and steps for the enterprise motion, are probably different and longer than what's required of the SMB motion. A single shared playbook in a Word document or long PowerPoint that needs to cater to the full sales team likely means a lot of overlapping sections and reps potentially getting confused reading sections that don't apply to them directly.

Now, there's an argument for seeing all your content in one place—it provides a complete picture or can support compliance, etc. But what if you could maintain the flow of a long-form document while *also* having the flexibility to update and deliver information in bite-sized, digestible chunks? This is the power of a modular content approach.

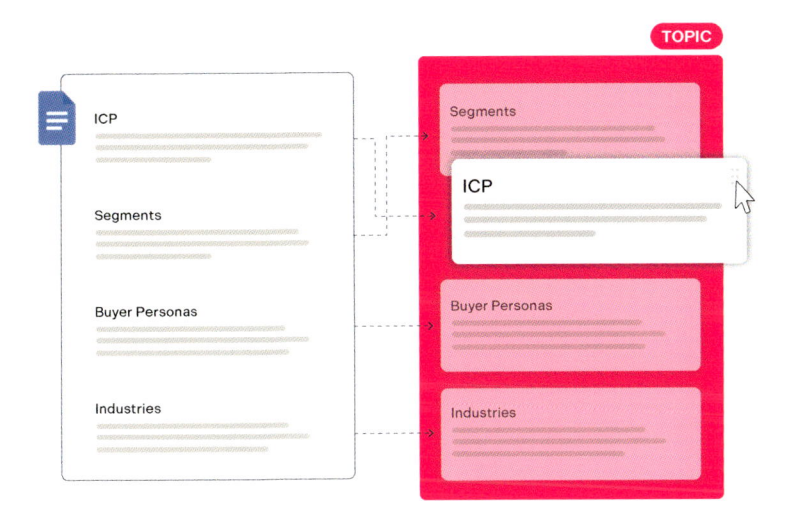

A new approach: modular and bite-sized

What if your content system worked like your favorite music streaming service? Just as Spotify lets you combine songs in different orders and create playlists for different moods or activities, a modern content system should allow you to assemble and reassemble bite-sized information into curated collections for specific purposes.

I've always loved the concept of playlists (I like to think that in another life, I was a DJ). I create playlists for different moods, different activities, and different times of day. And the ease of assembling and reassembling songs in different orders and for different purposes inspired my point of view on the future of enablement content design.

Modular content units

I envisioned modular content units (which we call "Speks" in our product) that could be assembled in any sequence, much like adding a song to any playlist. These modular content units could be assembled to form longer content pieces, such as a sales playbook, or create learning experiences, like product training. Collectively, these content units comprise a comprehensive knowledge base, data dictionary, and business glossary.

Think of a Spek as a "container" for content. It can hold anything from synced files, documents, or videos to a simple body of text. This allows organizations to support content as simple as a field definition or as robust as a case study.

As discussed in the previous chapter, this flexible content is paired with a flexible UX. The same piece of content could be viewed full screen in "learn mode," optimized for first-time learning, or embedded directly in the UI of one of your tools as a quick reference or as an answer to a question. This adaptability allows Speks to be used across the entire learning journey, from initial onboarding to ongoing skill development and performance support.

Each modular content unit is equipped with a powerful suite of enablement features, combining the best capabilities of traditional platforms. Users can share the content as they would with a CMS, test their understanding with a quick knowledge check like in an LMS, and even embed the content in their favorite tools like they would with a DAP.

The modular content units can then be dynamically assembled and reassembled into **Topics** just like you can organize songs in playlists. Unlike a traditional folder, which is just a dumping ground for files, a Topic provides structure and order. It's like a curated learning path, guiding users through a specific topic or process.

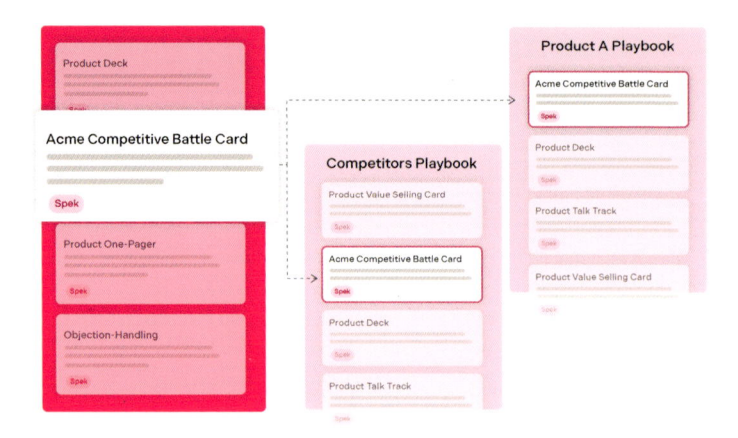

This also makes it easy to view all your related content in "one full picture," mimicking the experience of a long document but providing the benefits of small content pieces.

This comprehensive approach empowers users to interact with content meaningfully while providing administrators with granular analytics to track engagement and measure effectiveness. All of this is delivered through an intuitive and user-friendly interface.

Built for agility and constant change

This bite-sized approach to content isn't new. Forty-seven percent of teams planned to deploy some form of microlearning in 2024.[21] This modular, bite-sized approach offers a couple of key benefits:

- **Less repetition and duplication**: Organizations can reuse the same content in different contexts, eliminating redundancy and ensuring consistency. For example, that same product launch playbook can be used to onboard new hires, train existing reps on new features, and even support customer success teams.

- **Faster maintenance**: It also makes maintaining content accuracy infinitely easier. If a process changes or a product is updated, organizations only need to update the relevant Speks. The changes then automatically ripple through all the Topics that use those Speks.

- **More targeted change management**: By breaking content into smaller units, enablement professionals can send more targeted communications when processes change, track usage and engagement more effectively, identify knowledge gaps, and tailor enablement efforts to specific needs.

---

[21] LinkedIn. Workplace Learning Report. 2024. https://learning.linkedin.com/resources/workplace-learning-report

- **Personalized learning experience**: Chunking information into smaller pieces is more effective for knowledge retention. It also allows for greater personalization, as organizations can tailor content to specific roles, learning styles, and individual needs.

PRO TIP

Embrace bite-sized content today

Your reps are busy. Ditch long-form content and embrace the concept of microlearning and bite-sized content. Here's how:

1. Trade out lengthy blocks of text and long-winded explanations for bullet points, tables and rich text headers to create concise enablement materials, especially battlecards.

2. Need help getting started? **This is a great place to use AI**. Simply paste your existing enablement content into your company's AI provider of choice and use a prompt like:

"Please simplify this battlecard to be more bite-sized and easier to scan for our sales reps. Use bullet points, rich text formatting, and concise language."

3. For process documentation, use GIFs or short videos with screen recordings. Both are faster to create and more akin to the other content your reps consume (think social media habits).

For videos, remember, progress over perfection! Authenticity matters more than flawless delivery. A few stumbles make you human and encourage your reps to give it a try themselves. Besides, most recording tools allow you to cut out any part of the video in seconds. Free browser extensions simplify video recording, so don't let a lack of experience hold you back.

Your reps will thank you.

Connected content: A web of content powered by AI

Enablement teams need content that's not only bite-sized and easily reassembled, but also intuitively connected. This requires a content structure that moves beyond manual tagging and rigid folder structures, and instead exists as a dynamic, interconnected web of information.

Think of asking an AI assistant, "What are the key objections to our new product?" and instantly receiving a comprehensive response: a list of objections with direct links to relevant training materials, competitor comparisons, and customer testimonials. Further, imagine clicking on any term within that content (e.g., a product name, competitor, or acronym) and immediately accessing its definition, related resources, and more.

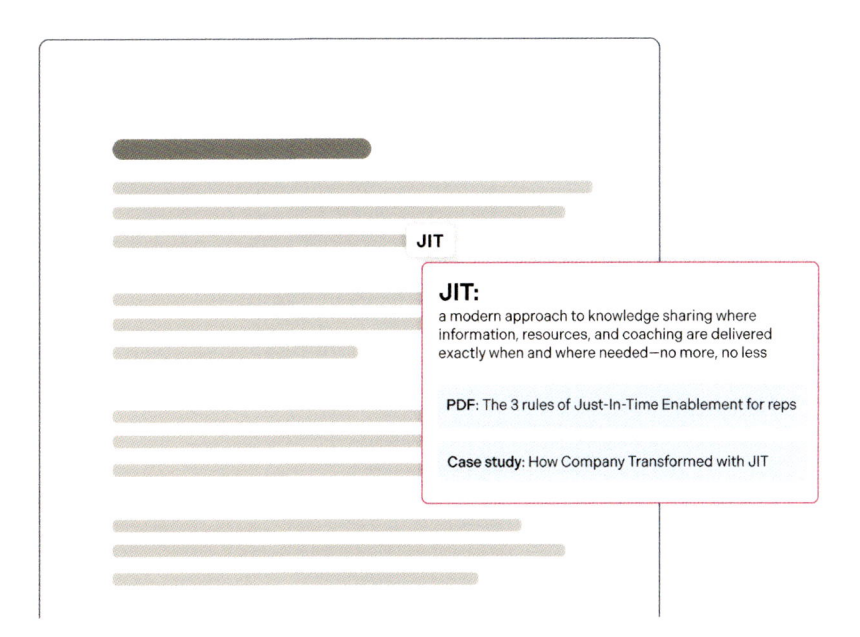

JIT

JIT:
a modern approach to knowledge sharing where information, resources, and coaching are delivered exactly when and where needed—no more, no less

PDF: The 3 rules of Just-In-Time Enablement for reps

Case study: How Company Transformed with JIT

AI makes this possible, connecting information without the cumbersome need for manual linking and tagging. Two key technologies make this possible: knowledge graphs and vector databases.

- **Knowledge graphs**: These define relationships between different entities, such as people, places, products, or any other domain-relevant concept. This allows you to easily connect information from disparate sources. Think of it as mapping the relationships between a song, artist, album, and record label within a music streaming service.

- **Vector knowledge**: These store individual pieces of knowledge represented as "vectors." Vectors capture the *semantic* meaning and context of the information, going beyond simple keyword matching. This enables the system to understand the *meaning* of the content, not just the words. This is how music streaming services can recommend a "summer vibes" playlist even if the songs aren't explicitly tagged as "summer." The vector database recognizes the semantic similarity in the music's characteristics.

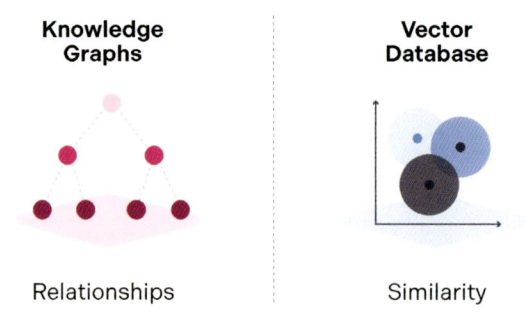

Knowledge Graphs — Relationships

Vector Database — Similarity

Combining knowledge graphs and vector databases unlocks powerful new possibilities for enablement.

Let's illustrate with an example. A knowledge graph might link a specific product feature to related training materials and sales plays. A vector database, meanwhile, could identify case studies featuring customers with similar needs, even if those case studies don't explicitly mention the product feature. By integrating these technologies, the system can surface highly relevant content that might otherwise be missed, such as a case study about a customer with similar needs and a training video that addresses a specific objection related to that need. This intelligent linking dramatically improves content discoverability and empowers enablement teams to quickly find the resources they need.

Understanding the relationship between different pieces of knowledge also unlocks a path to more effective, consistent and accurate content. If an update is made to a document, the system can automatically identify similar or related content that might need updated and automatically propagate the update throughout the system, eliminating the risk of outdated or conflicting information.

In fact, that was the inspiration for the original Spekit logo. Zari designed the original Spekit logo eight years ago with interconnected nodes to represent the very essence of continuous knowledge flow—individual pieces of information dynamically connecting and evolving.

A living ecosystem of knowledge

A flat, interconnected content architecture transforms information from a static collection of documents into a living, breathing ecosystem of knowledge. Just as Agile and modular design revolutionized software development, this unified and granular approach to content unlocks greater flexibility, adaptability, and personalization.

However, the true potential of AI extends far beyond linking concepts and improving content structure. AI can also play a crucial role in content curation and governance, helping us tackle the most significant challenge of content: decay.

In this chapter, we've explored the benefits of a unified platform and a modular approach to content. Next, let's dive deeper into the critical issue of content decay and how AI-powered dynamic content can provide the solution.

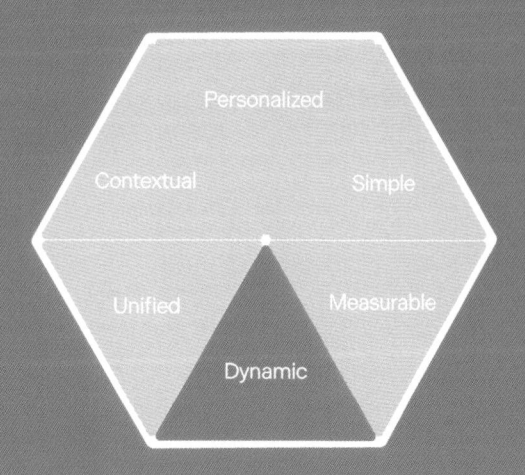

CHAPTER 8

The future of content is dynamic

HIGHLIGHTS

Uncover the hidden costs of outdated content and why traditional approaches to content management are failing.

Discover why most companies struggle with change management and how a focus on change enablement can bridge the gap. Explore how AI can proactively detect and prevent content decay, ensuring your enablement program always delivers accurate information.

Envision a future where your content is dynamically created and updated based on the insights gathered from all the tools your team uses.

I remember listening to a call recording from a key deal we ultimately lost. The prospect offered valuable product feedback, but I cringed when I heard our rep incorrectly answer a critical question. He'd missed a recent product update announcing the *very* capability the customer asked about and had relied, instead, on outdated talking points.

I gave feedback to the rep and their manager, directing them to our internal resource on the new capability, created just a month prior.

In return, they pointed out *three* battlecards that still referenced the old information. An absolute facepalm moment.

In this case, outdated content cost us the deal. In others, it could lead to customer churn or compliance risks.

Content decay: The silent killer of enablement

Content decay

Content decay represents the gradual decline in the relevance, accuracy, and usefulness of your content over time.

Content decay is the Achilles' heel of any enablement solution, no matter how sophisticated. Outdated, inaccurate, and duplicated information undermines sales efforts, frustrates teams, and erodes trust. As of January 2025, over half of marketing and enablement teams believe that 40-60% of their content needs a refresh, with 16.5% believing that up to 60-100% of their content is out of date. That's a lot of potentially wrong information their teams are relying on.[22]

Information becomes outdated in two primary ways: 1) through the addition of conflicting new information, or 2) when the underlying process or related information changes, regardless of whether new documentation is added.

Keeping content fresh and accurate is a constant, manual battle—an already unmanageable problem that's only intensifying. Reps' ever-changing needs, the evolving competitive landscape, and the rapid pace of product development and process changes make content curation increasingly difficult. The content management problem is ripe for disruption and demands a new solution.

> **Keeping content fresh and accurate is a constant, manual battle—an already unmanageable problem that's only intensifying.**

This chapter explores the main causes of content decay, from ineffective change enablement to the disconnect between content and the "source of truth," and how AI can provide a revolutionary approach.

Reason #1 for content decay: Broken change enablement

---

[22] Spekit. Spekit and Sales Enablement Collective Impact of Enablement Report 2025. Available at: https://www.spekit.com/impact-of-enablement-report

Despite all the discussion around change management, most companies aren't very good at it; it's not just the ones you've worked at!

Change management is a top concern I hear from executives, from Fortune 500 giants to cutting-edge tech firms. Even with formal centers of excellence (COE) or organizational change management (OCM) departments, it feels like everyone's improvising. There's no consistent, widely adopted standard.

When change isn't managed effectively, content is left behind, becoming stale and useless. Ineffective change management is a key driver of content decay.

Here's the problem: We're obsessed with *launching* changes, not enabling them. I would estimate that 90% of our energy goes into planning the implementation, which includes designing the change, product briefs, launch lists, and sprints—the mechanics of getting something out the door. Dozens of project management tools are designed to help you do just that. But what about updating all the existing documentation that is now out of date? That's the last item on anyone's list—or worse, it's not on anyone's list at all.

> Here's the problem: We're obsessed with *launching* changes, not enabling them.

When I ask leaders, "Do you have a repeatable, consistent **change enablement** process that your team follows and understands?" I'm often met with blank stares and awkward silence. Here's my definition of change enablement:

Change enablement

Change enablement encompasses all the steps—from documentation and training to communication and reinforcement—that you take to help people successfully adapt to and adopt change within an organization.

Think of it as the "human side" of change management. While change management often focuses on processes and procedures for implementing change, change enablement *focuses on the people affected* by those changes.

Change enablement, the crucial "how" that ensures that changes stick, gets a measly 5-10% (if that!) of the brain space in most projects. And significantly less of the budget.

95%
Change management

5%
Change enablement

This imbalance is striking, particularly when you compare it with the costs of the overall projects at stake. Even when organizations are millions of dollars deep into investing in CRMs like Salesforce, they often struggle to justify even a small fraction of that spend on change enablement. That's how much of an afterthought change adoption is.

Early in Spekit's journey, we often positioned our solution as an "insurance policy" for an organization's technology investments. For a customer focused on tool adoption, we'd explain that less than 3% of their overall CRM budget could ensure proper rep training and effective change management. This small investment could protect the much larger CRM investment from being undermined by poor training and ineffective change management. By framing Spekit's cost as a percentage of their existing Salesforce budget, we were essentially highlighting how little they were currently allocating to the very thing that would make their CRM successful: effective change enablement. When executives saw the cost in that context, the value proposition became much clearer.

Managing "micro-changes": an impossible task

While companies may have more structured change enablement processes for what I call "macro-changes"—the big splashy initiatives like sales methodology or CRM rollouts—they often overlook the "micro-changes" that affect daily work. These small changes include the minor process updates, new fields, and revised battlecards that constantly crop up. No consistent communication strategy exists. One week, it's an email; the next, it's a Slack message; sometimes, it's forgotten altogether.

Even when the change is communicated, documentation rarely gets updated. CRM documentation is a prime example. It's a common and frustrating problem, as CRM documentation often becomes outdated the moment a change is made to the platform. I experienced this firsthand while managing Salesforce documentation at RealtyShares. Our "source of truth" spreadsheet, affectionately nicknamed "The Beast," contained all our field definitions and other crucial information. But even after a major audit and initial documentation effort, manually tracking every Salesforce change and updating that spreadsheet proved impossible. It quickly became inaccurate and unwieldy.

Competitive and product enablement materials, along with other sales enablement content, face the same risk of decay.

While I believe this problem is nearly impossible to solve relying solely on humans, there are practical steps you can take now, even without advanced technology, to mitigate the challenge of content decay.

PRO TIP

Create a repeatable change enablement process

To ensure consistency and efficiency in your enablement efforts, design a repeatable process that aligns with the scale of the change. A simple "T-shirt sizing" approach can help you determine the appropriate level of effort and the combination of tactics to employ.

Step 1: Align on "T-shirt" size definitions for your various types of changes.

Size	Examples	Enablement Approach
S	New field added to CRM, minor process update, new blog post published	Focus on quick, lightweight communication and reinforcement
M	New product one-pager, updated battlecard, minor feature release	Combine just-in-time guidance with readily accessible resources
L	Major process update, significant feature launch	Combine just-in-time guidance with more structured learning and reinforcement
XL	CRM migration, new tool implementation, new sales methodology	A comprehensive strategy combining in-person workshops, lots of communications leading up to the change, user acceptance testing (UAT) groups, structured learning and just-in-time reinforcement

Step 2: Align on the steps taken for various types of changes.

Size	Live Training	Course	Documen-tation	Chat/Email Comms
S				X
M			X	X
L		X	X	X
XL	X	X	X	X

Of course, this list can be expanded to include other communication and training methods, such as all-hands meetings, weekly updates, asynchronous mini-courses, assessments, and more. The key is to tailor the approach to your specific needs and maintain consistency across similar initiatives.

Step 3: Communicate this framework (and make it easily accessible) to your entire team to ensure alignment.

By establishing a clear framework for your enablement efforts, you can ensure consistency, streamline your workflow, and maximize the impact of your initiatives.

Since I love this topic, before we continue on content decay, here are a few more quick tips.

PRO TIP

Change management dos and don'ts

Effective change management is crucial for driving adoption and minimizing disruption. Here's a handy guide to ensure your change communications are clear, consistent, and impactful:

Don't	Do
Don't leave documentation to be an afterthought	Do make "updating documentation" a required step in your change management or release process: • Include a stage in Jira or your project management tool that requires updating product enablement as part of any release
Don't wait until the 11th hour to announce key changes. Establish a regular communication schedule to keep your team informed and prepared.	Do establish a consistent communication schedule to keep your team informed and provide opportunities for questions and support. For example: • Bi-weekly Wednesday AM change communications • Thursday PM office hours
Don't bombard your team with fragmented messages across multiple channels. This creates confusion and distraction. For example: • Important! New fields in SFDC • Update to CPQ. Please read!	Do develop a template for your change communications in a consistent, consolidated format. Do use a consistent naming convention for your release communications (i.e. email subject lines) so that they're easy to search for when your reps need them. For example: **SFDC Release - [Date] - [Description]** • SFDC Release - 05/10/23 - New CPQ Fields

Don't	Do
Don't send vague or incomplete communications: "On 12/1/21, we're adding a new Finance-required field – ARR – to the Opportunity"	Do provide clear explanations that answer the "why," "who," "what," and "when" of the change: *"To pay you and other AEs correctly and on time, a new field called 'ARR' is being added to the Opportunity object. Starting Monday 12/1/21, you'll need to fill out the ARR field when you 'Close Won' a new deal"*
Don't wait until after the change is rolled out to solicit feedback from the field.	Do have a UAT group and champions forum.
Don't "say it and forget it"	Do create Slack or Teams channels and email groups for questions: • #ProductFAQ • #SalesforceFAQ • #CPQ FAQ Do host regular office hours. Do measure engagement and communicate results . Do highlight victories with shout-outs in channels. Do share the wins in team and company meetings. For big changes, give recognition and awards.

Reason #2: Nobody gets fired for outdated documentation

The other reason your content is outdated? Lack of ownership. Rarely is anyone *genuinely held accountable* for keeping content up to date - especially process documentation.

Or, if the wrong department "owns" it, it's likely to fall by the wayside as well. I've seen this play out countless times. Eager IT teams purchase a DAP with the narrow goal of driving tool adoption, usually tied to a big CRM or configure, price, quote software (CPQ) rollout. A flurry of activity around documentation and training occurs during these projects. But once the tool is live, that focus vanishes, and eventually, the content goes stale, and the platform's value falls short.

Why? Misaligned priorities and lack of context are common culprits. IT and CRM teams often prioritize feature launches over training—ironically leading to more time spent on user support than on proactive documentation. Furthermore, these teams, and even L&D, often lack the business process context needed to create truly effective enablement content. Enablement teams, with their understanding of employee needs, workflows, and the nuances of driving adoption, are better suited for this task.

Reason #3: Ineffective mechanisms to prevent decay

The truth is, we're set up to fail. Even with the best intentions and workflows, identifying every piece of content needing an update after a change is impossible. We're fighting a losing battle against systems not designed for continuous knowledge maintenance.

> Even with the best intentions and workflows, identifying every piece of content needing an update after a change is impossible.

Simply throwing more people at the problem won't fix it.

Most enablement and content platforms offer features that promise to help with content governance, including expiration dates, experts, verified by features, approval processes, and more. But do these features solve the problem? The sad truth is that these demo-friendly features rarely deliver. They create an illusion of control without addressing the core issue.

Sure, you can set an arbitrary date in the future to remind you to verify content. You might base this on your best guess of a long enough timelapse or a regulatory timeframe. That may help. But ultimately, you'll still need to review that content manually. You're choosing to give homework to your future self, hoping that on a randomly selected day in the future, you'll have the time to verify an article or sales sheet.

You'll repeat this process for the next few dozen of processes, products, competitive updates, and other rollouts.

Before you know it, you and your team will wake up to endless to-do lists for verifying content. Even then, relying on individual content creators to catch every error or update every document is a recipe for disaster.

Maybe you'll update some of them. But have you really escaped the endless cycle of content decay? And do you have any time left at the end of the day after constantly cleaning up content to focus on the more strategic enablement items that drive growth and actually matter?

The real question we should be asking is: **In a world where AI can analyze and categorize content in realtime, do we need these archaic capabilities at all?**

Take tags, for example. While essential, tags have long been a content creator's nemesis, consuming countless hours from the struggle of inventing consistent naming conventions to manually tagging each resource. And despite all of these efforts, sales reps still struggle to find what they need for any given deal. To solve this, some platforms offer the option of manually mapping CRM fields to tags so that you can surface content based on opportunity and account criteria. But the process is so tedious and prone to errors that it's almost comical.

I believe that many of these traditional content management capabilities will soon be obsolete.

Accuracy in a world of AI

This issue of accuracy becomes even more insidious in the age of AI copilots or chatbots. While these weren't around in 2017 when I was looking for a solution, they are quickly becoming part of the standard enablement stack.

These digital assistants promise to revolutionize knowledge sharing with their ability to answer questions by searching all your content systems.

However, while a seemingly perfect solution, AI chatbots often become just another destination in the cluttered landscape of enablement tools. More concerning is that reps, accustomed to instant answers, understandably expect the information that these tools provide to be accurate without knowing if it is.

What happens when the chatbot confidently answers a sales rep's question with outdated pricing information? Or worse, when two internal documents offer conflicting guidance on product specifications?

Thirty-one percent of sales teams cited that their biggest obstacle to adoption of AI was incomplete, inaccurate, or old data, and that only

55% of business buyers trust AI to be as accurate as a human.[23]

Initially swept up in the fervor of LLMs and ChatGPT, organizations are now realizing that connecting a chatbot to their content is the first step. AI cannot magically transform bad content into good insights.

The "garbage in, garbage out" problem

The truth is that these AI chatbots are simply an improved UX layer on top of the same content systems we've discussed. They are only as good as the data they are trained on. Sure, LLMs can scan vast amounts of content to generate answers quickly, but those answers' accuracy depends on the content quality. If the underlying content is outdated, inaccurate, or contradictory, the AI will amplify these flaws, delivering "garbage" outputs. Unless the source content is kept up to date (which it likely wasn't), the AI is more likely to provide an inaccurate answer—and the rep may have been better off asking their manager the question on Slack. Hence the phrase, "*garbage in, garbage out*."

Let's break this down in the context of an AI-powered enablement platform:

Garbage In
This is the information that lives in the system. If content is outdated, inaccurate, or inconsistent, AI tools will be relying on flawed knowledge.

Garbage Out
This is the AI's response. Even the most sophisticated AI cannot generate accurate insights if the underlying information is flawed.

Many AI solutions, especially the "plug-and-play" solutions that connect to your existing content, focus on solving the "garbage out" problem

---

23 Salesforce. State of Sales. 2024. Available at: https://www.salesforce.com/resources/research-reports/state-of-sales/

by improving search. Their value proposition hinges on developing sophisticated algorithms to sift through information and display the most relevant results.

While these advancements are valuable, they address only part of the challenge. That's because effective enablement isn't just about finding answers. It's about ensuring that your entire enablement program, including all the content leveraged, is current and aligned with business objectives.

Even if your search engine improves what happens to the outdated presentations you're still using to onboard new hires? Or the one-pager your CSMs are sending to customers that reflects last year's pricing?

That's why I believe preventing garbage out isn't enough. We need to prevent garbage from piling up *in* the system in the first place. We need to *proactively* prevent content decay.

> We need to prevent garbage from piling up in the system in the first place. We need to *proactively* prevent content decay.

AI: the guardian of content freshness

We need to move beyond finding the best needle in the haystack to *ensuring that the entire haystack is made of gold*.

AI can play a meaningful role in preventing garbage in the system —a task previously impossible for humans. Imagine having your very own AI-powered content curation assistant that could help you identify clashes between new information and existing content, instances where changes to underlying systems of record have rendered existing documentation outdated, or places in your sales motion where content is lacking.

Leveraging AI to identify content conflicts

As we explored in earlier chapters, using techniques like semantic similarity, this AI curation assistant could easily identify related information, opening the door to detect not only duplicate content but also conflicting information.

This is particularly helpful for catching clashes between new and old information, particularly when new content is being added to the system.

Let's revisit the example of outdated product information. What if upon adding the new content to your system, your AI curation assistant could instantly flag conflicting information in your battlecards and even draft revisions for your approval at that very moment?

This kind of proactive intervention would prevent inconsistency and errors before they affect your team's performance.

Leveraging AI to track system changes

My frustrating experience managing CRM documentation led me to envision a better way. What if, instead of treating documentation as separate from the system, we recognized that the CRM's data model itself is a reflection of the business? The fields, objects, and relationships within the CRM mirror the company's key elements: its products, competitors, sales stages, and more.

Therefore, documentation should be dynamically linked to this data model. When the CRM's data model changes—for example, when you add a new competitor or product—the documentation should automatically detect those changes and either alert us to update it or update itself. This approach ensures the documentation remains aligned with the evolving business, providing accurate and up-to-date information.

And, taking inspiration from DAPs, what if the system included built-in change communication workflows? This means automatically embedding the documentation directly within the CRM, right next to the relevant fields, and using in-app alerts and notifications to inform users of changes. Imagine this: when a change occurs, the relevant users are immediately notified within the application itself. No more juggling tools or manual processes.

This is the exact vision behind our unique approach to CRM integrations. But CRM documentation is just the start. I see a future where every piece of knowledge in your business is dynamically linked to its source of truth. Product knowledge could automatically track changes released into production by connecting to Jira or Github. When a new capability launches, the system could update existing product content or generate a draft of a product-value selling card for your review.

Leveraging AI to close content gaps

Real-time data will drive the future of content—data from your entire technology stack.

Of all the potential data sources fueling dynamic enablement content, I believe conversations hold the most potential.

Conversations capture invaluable, real-time insights, especially in areas like competitive intelligence, where changes happen rapidly. For example, competitive information regarding product functionality or pricing is often scarce or lagging. While you can find surface-level competitive information online, the most valuable insights usually come directly from sales conversations with prospects who are evaluating various solutions.

At Spekit, we experienced the power of real-time competitive insights in 2023 when we launched our content-tracking feature, SmartSend. We based our initial competitive pricing research on information we found online, which quickly became outdated as the market shifted. Our sales team, relying on this obsolete information, was caught off guard when customers cited competitor pricing up to 50% lower than we assumed. After enough reps mentioned it, we investigated and updated our content.

This experience highlights a common challenge: How often do representatives encounter new information on calls and not realize it's forming a pattern? My guess is often.

This is where AI can play an important role in ensuring your team has the most up-to-date information by identifying knowledge gaps and proactively closing them.

For example, imagine your AI-powered content curation assistant notices a new competitor frequently mentioned on sales calls, but your existing content on that competitor is sparse. To address this, it could automatically draft a comprehensive battlecard based on an analysis of publicly available information, past call interactions, and your existing competitive content. From that point on, it can listen for signals of updates, suggesting revisions based on new information uncovered on calls.

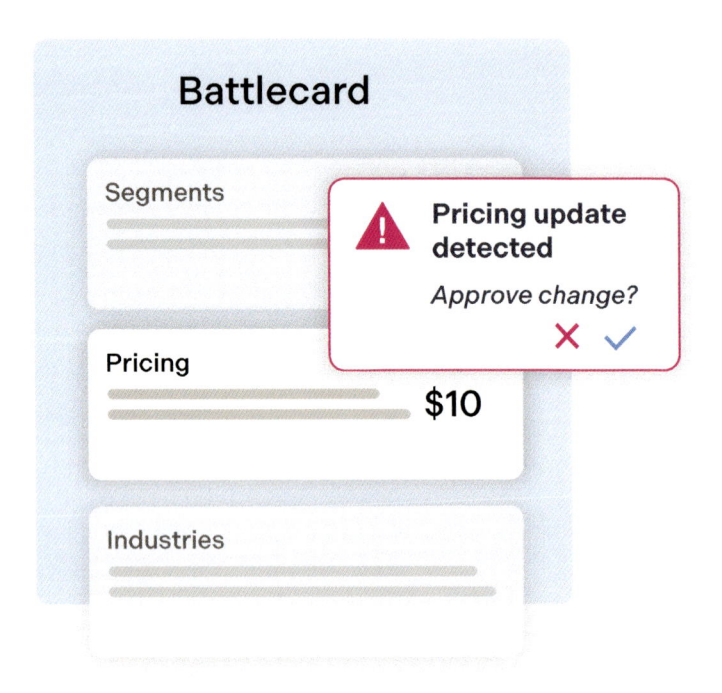

Leveraging AI to capture the collective intelligence of the field

Similarly, we can leverage AI to bridge a gap that has been a significant challenge for organizations: harnessing the field's collective intelligence.

Many organizations restrict content creation in their enablement platforms to a select few to maintain quality and control. But this approach often backfires. Many sales leaders, especially those with experienced teams, create content on the side, bypassing the official platform altogether. They develop their own templates, decks, messaging, and emails, often storing them in personal repositories and sharing them individually with their teams—adding to the content chaos. I don't believe they intend to undermine enablement teams' efforts; they simply want to use the information they view as most effective.

This presents an opportunity: How can we leverage the field's collective intelligence while maintaining content quality? AI again provides a solution. Instead of relying on intuition or guesswork, your AI curation assistant could analyze your sales calls, identifying and summarizing the most effective discovery questions, competitive insights, and objection-handling techniques that your top performers use.

The good news is that this isn't science fiction; it's the future of content curation—and it's coming quickly.

PRO TIP

Embrace AI-powered content curation tools

Become an expert in learning technologies and AI-powered content curation tools that can personalize the learning experience and provide real-time feedback.

As a reminder, if using any private company data (i.e. call recording transcript), ensure you're using a company-approved AI solution for data security reasons.

- **Play with AI writing tools**: Experiment with AI writing tools to generate different types of content. Try reformatting your enablement newsletter or even creating scripts for training videos. Pay attention to how these tools use language and structure information to learn how to improve your own writing.

- **Turn your live trainings into bite-sized reinforcement**: Repurpose your live training content. Upload recordings of Sales Weekly Meetings or enablement sessions and use AI to generate bite-sized reinforcement materials. Prompt the AI to analyze the transcript and identify key highlights, takeaways, and questions. (Many tools like Zoom and Teams now offer this functionality.) Similarly, record interviews with sales leaders or industry experts on key topics (like competitor insights) and use AI to transform those recordings into valuable enablement resources.

- **Test using your data to build better enablement**: Upload transcripts from your ten most successful discovery calls and prompt an AI tool with something like: 'Analyze these transcripts and identify the ten most important discovery questions our reps should be asking.' Experiment with this technique for other enablement needs, like creating battlecards or objection handling guides.

- **Build your own enablement prompt-library**: Just as I suggested keeping a prompt library for your reps, create one for your enablement team. Store your most successful prompts for generating things like battlecards, value selling cards, and training materials. This will help you create high-quality content consistently.

- **Test AI-powered video training**: While I've had my own reservations around the concept of AI avatars, tools like Synthesia can help you create high-quality training videos quickly.

- **Test AI-powered presentation tools**: Tools exist that can help you create professional presentations quickly. Experiment with these tools to see how they can save you time and improve the quality of your presentations.

Measurability: the foundation for continuous improvement

Throughout this chapter, we've explored the critical challenge of content decay and how dynamic, AI-powered content and curation assistants can provide the solution. But AI can do even more to ensure content's quality and effectiveness.

This brings us to the final pillar of the future of enablement: measurability. By tracking content usage and performance, we can gain valuable insights into what works, identify areas for improvement, and continuously optimize our enablement efforts.

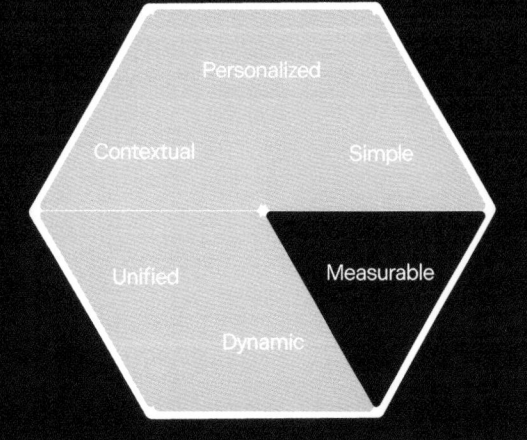

CHAPTER 9

The future of content is measurable

HIGHLIGHTS

Discover why traditional enablement metrics fall short and how a new approach to measurement is needed.

Uncover the challenges of proving the ROI of enablement and why a shift in focus is necessary.

Explore how Just-In-Time Enablement unlocks valuable insights into content usage, rep performance, and knowledge gaps.

Learn how AI can help identify trends, optimize content, and demonstrate the true value of enablement.

We've reimagined the future of enablement with unified platforms and dynamic, AI-powered content delivered just-in-time to reps. But now, a critical question emerges: Can we finally accomplish the holy grail of enablement and measure the "return on investment (ROI)" of enablement?

> Can we finally accomplish the holy grail of enablement and measure the "ROI" of enablement?

This question haunts many enablement and marketing leaders. We pour our hearts into creating content, designing playbooks, and delivering training sessions, but proving their direct influence on revenue often seems impossible. How can you prove that a 30-minute lesson made a rep feel more prepared for a competitive deal weeks later? Can you directly attribute an increase in win rates to last month's competitor training?

Sure, you can probably create a slide or two with vanity metrics on completion rates and training attendance rates. But can you prove that any of that matters? Not only do these metrics fail to capture the true effect of enablement, but most organizations aren't even tracking their work in the first place.

It's time to move beyond gut feelings and vanity metrics to truly understand enablement's impact. In this chapter, we'll explore how Just-In-Time Enablement is a data-driven approach that can unlock the insights we need to optimize content, improve rep performance, and demonstrate enablement's real value once and for all.

The fallacy of ROI

Let's be honest: Measuring the ROI of any enablement investment, including technology, has always been tricky. It's often a matter of a gut feeling or anecdotal reporting—you either have an initiative or platform that your team loves and finds valuable, or you don't.

But this challenge isn't unique to enablement. It's similar to trying to measure the ROI of Salesforce, Zoom, or even Uber. These tools provide immense value, but that value often transcends easy metrics and simple calculations.

While I can't tell you the precise ROI of Uber, as someone who takes over 50 flights per year, I know it saves me time and, more importantly, reduces headaches when navigating a new city - and that is invaluable to me. Similarly, I can't quantify the ROI of the conversation intelligence tool our sales team uses, but the value it provides—from capturing customer feedback to identifying coaching opportunities—is undeniable.

Frankly, I think the whole concept of proving ROI in enablement with regard to "revenue impact" has been mostly a marketing gimmick, at least until recently. It's designed to give you a comforting illusion of measurability rather than providing actionable insights.

Take the classic example of many CMS platforms: "Tie buyer engagement data to revenue impact." While understanding buyer engagement to drive more effective content is valuable, this idea that a potential customer glancing at a case study for two minutes directly translates to "influenced revenue" is misleading. The number itself is often arbitrary, with little connection to real-world outcomes.

Simply too many intertwined factors influence whether a rep wins a deal. If every tool we purchased delivered on the 30% more pipeline and 25% more productivity it promised, we'd all be doing billions in revenue with just three reps!

Similarly, proving a direct correlation between training and winning a deal is difficult because of the time lag between when reps learn something and when it's applied in the field. Weeks or months may pass, making it nearly impossible to draw a definitive connection.

But, I think there is a world ahead where measuring true business impact is possible.

Operating in the dark

When I ask sales leaders who are hesitant to invest in a dedicated enablement platform: "What knowledge, when mastered, has the greatest effect on ramp time," they often admit that they simply don't know. Their responses usually reveal an unsurprising yet concerning truth: Many companies lack visibility into their reps' needs. Instead, they rely solely on retroactive analysis once teams miss quotas or goals.

Most organizations today operate in the dark, struggling to understand what truly drives rep performance.

> Most organizations today operate in the dark, struggling to understand what truly drives rep performance.

Sales, enablement, and marketing leaders grapple with questions such as:

- Which skills are most crucial for success?
- What knowledge, when mastered, has the greatest effect on ramp time?
- What training programs have the greatest effect on performance?
- What content leads to better outcomes?

- Where do reps need the most coaching?
- What content is outdated and underutilized?
- What content is truly driving results?

Even when some visibility exists, it's often fragmented and incomplete due to the enablement landscape's disjointed nature. This makes it incredibly difficult to get a complete picture.

The demand for clear insights

Do the answers to these questions not matter to sales leaders? Of course they do.

But here's the kicker: In the fall of 2024, we interviewed 25 vice presidents of sales/chief revenue officers. Guess how many admitted to regularly logging into their enablement platforms where some of these answers exist? Only two! Several had *never* logged in.

While this small sample size isn't statistically significant, it mirrors the results in the 2025 Impact of Enablement Survey[24] that showed that 74.2% of enablement teams believe their sales leader has logged into their enablement platform five times or less (or they don't even know!) in the last quarter. At best, that's once every three weeks. This raises a critical question: Are enablement platforms truly serving sales leaders' needs?

The truth is that getting sales leadership buy-in for enablement is a constant challenge. Top-down reinforcement is often lacking, but even I was surprised by the extent of this disconnect.

Interestingly, guess what the number-one favorite tool was across those same sales leaders? Clari—a revenue forecasting tool with dashboards

---

24 Spekit. Spekit and Sales Enablement Collective Impact of Enablement Report 2025. Available at: https://www.spekit.com/impact-of-enablement-report

that provide pipeline insights. The second was Salesforce dashboards and reports, followed closely by Gong, which offers insights into sales conversations.

Many leaders said they logged into Clari or Salesforce daily. When asked why they didn't rely on reports from sales ops or managers, they cited a desire to "dig in" and identify gaps and patterns themselves.

So, here's the disconnect: Sales leaders crave performance insights, yet they rarely use the platforms designed to provide those insights!

My hunch is that this is because enablement platforms are missing the mark when it comes to delivering valuable insights that resonate with sales leaders. And many leaders are simply unaware of the powerful insights available to them.

PRO TIP

Enable your sales leaders on your data

Don't forget about your sales leaders! While much of the focus is often on enabling reps, it's crucial to educate your revenue leaders and managers on the valuable insights available within your enablement platform.

To make these insights even more accessible, consider sending a weekly highlights email summarizing key trends and takeaways from your enablement data. This keeps leaders informed, promotes data-driven decision-making, and reinforces your enablement program's value.

Here are just a few examples of insights that might matter to revenue leaders:

Analytics	Insight for Revenue Leaders
Content recommendations analytics	If the same content or theme keeps getting recommended, it's likely that the theme is coming up a lot in rep conversations, and additional enablement may be required.
Content usage analytics	Understand which resources are most helpful at each stage of the sales cycle and identify the content gaps that hinder deal progression. Identify top-performing content that drives desired behaviors (e.g., content related to objection handling that correlates with higher win rates).
Search and answers analytics	Identify knowledge gaps affecting deal cycles (e.g., frequent searches for pricing information may indicate a need for more precise pricing documentation) and pinpoint areas where reps require additional training or coaching. Uncover trends related to new product launches or market changes. Is a specific competitor spiking in your search trends? You might need to pay more attention to them. Is no one searching for your new product? You might need to reinforce and make sure your reps are selling it.
Team engagement analytics	Gain a holistic view of rep performance, including knowledge levels, content engagement, and sales outcomes, and compare them across your teams. Facilitate data-driven coaching conversations and performance reviews.

Individual rep engagement analytics	Identify skill or will. If the content is there but your reps aren't using it, you can determine if performance issues stem from a lack of knowledge (skill) or a lack of motivation/execution (will). Identify reps who may require additional support or coaching in specific areas to tailor interventions to address individual needs and improve overall team performance.
Top performers	Understand what your top performers are doing to prepare before calls, follow up on deals, etc. so you can coach your other reps.

Fragmented data, fragmented insights

The reality is, enablement's fragmented nature today makes getting a clear picture of "what's working" incredibly challenging. Just as scattered enablement platforms create content chaos, scattered data creates insights chaos. And the rise of AI will only amplify this problem.

Every revenue technology and CRM platform is leaping onto the AI search and content bandwagon, each promising their latest chatbot will be the magic bullet for your content woes.

Salesforce is a prime example. They've tried tackling the enablement challenge before with MyTrailhead, then Sales Enablement, then Sales Programs. Now, it's Einstein's turn, promising to magically connect to SharePoint and solve all your problems. (While I'm poking a little fun at Salesforce here, I wouldn't underestimate their commitment to AI under Marc Benioff's leadership).

And if it's not one of the tech giants, it's your IT team, convinced their latest internal AI chatbot will finally solve all your enablement headaches. But, as we explored earlier, simple questions like "How do you rank conflicting resources?" or "How are you helping sales leaders understand rep needs?" quickly expose the limitations of these homegrown solutions.

Connecting a chatbot to your content is just the beginning. Try getting those internally built chatbots to provide the reporting and insights you actually need. First, your dev team would have to add all the necessary tracking, build the queries, and create the dashboards. But wait, reps are complaining about hallucinations—now they need to tweak the ranking algorithm. The result? That data request gets buried in the ever-growing backlog, leaving you with a tool that may not even be giving correct answers, and you have no way to prove it. Sound familiar? Development resources are precious; are they really best spent on reinventing the wheel?

The problem with partial insights

Even if these platforms deliver on their promises, they still only represent a fraction of where your reps work. The result? Reps juggling ten different chat interfaces across all their tools, making it virtually impossible to gain any real visibility into what's actually happening.

Each tool's chatbot has its own proprietary RAG system, recommendation engine, ranking algorithms, and its own partial dataset. While this might work for tool-specific questions (e.g., using the "ASK" feature in your call intelligence tool to ask, "What were my buyer's biggest concerns on the last call?"), it falls short for general enablement questions. Each platform only has a sliver of insight into your reps' content usage, analyzed and recommended by its own unique (and limited) algorithm.

This fragmented approach makes it incredibly difficult to get a complete picture of your enablement efforts and what's actually driving performance. In a world increasingly reliant on AI, a centralized source of truth for your enablement data will be essential for accurate insights and an optimal rep experience.

Just-In-Time Enablement: The key to measurable impact

This is why I'm so passionate about the key differentiator of Just-In-Time Enablement: its contextual nature. By spanning the entire rep experience, Just-In-Time Enablement unlocks a world of previously inaccessible data.

By working everywhere the rep works, Just-In-Time Enablement provides unprecedented visibility into how reps use content in real-world scenarios. We can see exactly what they were doing when they accessed specific information, providing valuable context for understanding its impact.

The approach also provides centralized analytics regardless of how or where the rep accesses it. The result is a single source of truth for all your enablement data, eliminating fragmented insights.

This holistic view empowers data-driven decision-making, revealing which content is most helpful, which reps engage with it, and how enablement efforts affect rep performance. And, of course, all of this content engagement data can be used for better personalization, tailoring enablement experiences to each rep's needs and performance goals.

Perhaps most importantly, Just-In-Time Enablement offers a path to more meaningful measurement. While proving the ROI of enablement has historically been challenging, this approach allows us to minimize the time between when information is consumed and when it is applied. This maximizes the chances of correlation and provides a clearer understanding of what drives rep performance.

Call centers show the value

Just-In-Time Enablement is already proving its worth in call centers, where data-driven decision-making is paramount. Call centers are notoriously metrics-driven, often piloting new solutions before they buy them to prove that they will directly reduce costs or increase revenue.

For example, we have an aviation customer with more than 4,000 call center reps who use Spekit to access answers on the fly while resolving customer issues. We analyzed ticket resolution times and discovered that the agents using Spekit decreased the lengths of their interactions by 20% compared with those not using our solution. The most impressive part? The call center achieved these results before we even offered our AI-powered search experience. Providing the right information at the right time, within the flow of work, reduced how often the call center agents had to access information in SharePoint or get support from their peers or managers, thus saving time and money.

I believe this same level of measurability is possible for sales reps. Imagine a rep receiving a personalized content recommendation right after a call where a prospect expresses interest in a specific product capability. Their AI enablement assistant could then track whether the rep reviews the content and its effect on subsequent interactions (e.g., did the next call move the deal forward, did the opportunity move to the next stage, etc.), providing real-time measurement of content effectiveness.

Gaps and trends

While tracking content usage and understanding what's working is helpful, **proactively identifying enablement or rep performance gaps** is way more powerful in improving sales performance and acquiring sales leadership buy-in.

Today, identifying these gaps often depends on proactive hand-raising from reps or managers, deciphering noise in Slack, compiling data, and other manual processes that involve time-consuming field surveys. (See the next chapter for some practical guidance.) There's frequently a significant time lag between when the gap is first identified and when it's surfaced to sales leadership, enablement, and marketing.

But Just-In-Time Enablement can help identify gaps in real-time.

For example, the previously mentioned aviation company also leverages their built-in dashboards in Spekit around search data (trending searches, searches with no results, searches with no click-throughs) to get real-time visibility into emerging customer issues and potential knowledge gaps, allowing them to respond quickly and effectively.

And when a critical update needs to be communicated immediately, they can push that notification directly into the apps the reps are using, maximizing awareness and instantly tracking readership across their entire workforce. This allows the company to identify any gaps where employees might be at risk of being unprepared.

Similarly, by analyzing patterns in the questions that your sales team asks or context patterns extracted from conversations, you can start to identify themes around your reps' needs and the enablement that could help.

But you can also identify what is working. For example, by understanding and analyzing your top-performing new hires' content consumption patterns, you can reveal the "most effective" content for onboarding and productivity.

For example, imagine seeing which enablement content your strongest sales development representatives (SDRs) are reviewing. What if you discovered that your top-performing SDRs aren't spending more time mastering discovery questions and talk tracks but instead are focused on value-selling cards and product enablement? How would that influence your onboarding program or the coaching your managers provide?

These sorts of trends allow you to optimize training programs for future recruits—accelerating their time to productivity—and give your sales leaders and managers powerful visibility into focus areas.

Leveraging AI for insights

Let's take a common example of AI using the context of your sales conversations to surface content. That same mechanism can also identify gaps in your knowledge base. (While a Just-In-Time Enablement platform may not store the specific contexts of individual conversations for security purposes, the aggregated insights can be incredibly valuable).

For example, say your Just-In-Time Enablement assistant notices a recurring context theme in your sales conversations—pricing-related objections.

With a just-in-time platform, you can track how often reps access pricing-related content during these conversations and whether that content helps them overcome objections. If a particular piece of content is consistently underperforming, you can identify the gap and proactively update or replace it.

Here's how this might work in practice:

1. **Contextual analysis**: The AI analyzes sales conversations and identifies recurring themes, such as "pricing objections" or "competitor comparisons."
2. **Content recommendation**: Based on these themes, the AI recommends relevant content to reps in real time.

3. **Performance tracking**: The platform tracks whether reps access the recommended content.

4. **Gap identification**: If the recommended content isn't getting used or has a low relevancy score, the AI flags a potential gap in your knowledge base and even creates a draft for you to review to close it.

This AI-powered gap analysis allows you to proactively address knowledge gaps, improve content quality, and ensure your team always has the information they need to succeed.

Insights will divide the winners and losers

As the examples above showcase, the value of Just-In-Time Enablement goes beyond simply delivering knowledge in the moment of need for reps. It becomes a powerful tool for gathering data, identifying patterns, and generating insights that can revolutionize how we understand and optimize employee performance.

By directly measuring enablement content's effect on actions and outcomes, organizations can finally unlock their investments' true value.

Many unknowns still exist, but the truth is stark: **The winners and losers in today's data-driven world will be divided by one factor— their ability to harness the power of information.** The organizations that can unlock the insights hidden within their data will be the ones that grow. Meanwhile, those that cling to outdated methods, and fail to embrace this future of AI-powered Just-In-Time Enablement will struggle to keep up.

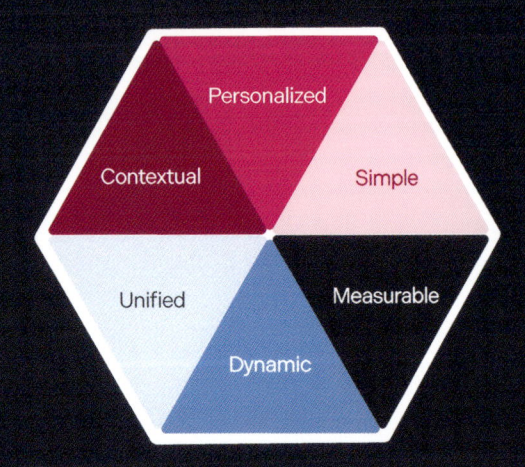

CHAPTER 10

Preparing for the future

HIGHLIGHTS

Discover how AI will evolve the role of enablement with a focus on higher-level activities.

Learn about how performance architects, a new role for this new era, can provide strategic insights and data-driven guidance to sales teams.

Explore five actions you can take today to ready your enablement for an era of AI and ensure buy-in from your organization's leadership.

Understand the urgency behind enablement information and why organizations that don't adapt will be left behind.

The future of work is being rewritten before our very eyes, and AI is holding the pen. If you've read this far, you're not just witnessing this transformation—you're ready to lead it.

While some of the concepts we've explored are still years away or may remain in the realm of our imagination, many are possible today or will soon become the new normal.

This isn't just a glimpse into what *might* be; it's a **call to action** for what *must* be. AI-powered, Just-In-Time Enablement is key to the future of sales, and the individuals and companies that embrace it first will dominate. The question isn't if this will happen, but whether you will seize the advantage.

This book has explored the "why" of this revolution. But before we close out this journey together, let's tackle the crucial questions that will shape your success in this new era:

- **What does the future of the enablement role look like?**
- **How can organizations drive buy-in and create a culture of shared ownership in enablement?**

The ugly truth

Let's address the elephant in the room: Will AI render the enablement role obsolete?

No. But it will fundamentally change it. Frankly, this change is a necessity for the survival of enablement as a strategic function.

The ugly truth is that enablement is still too often undervalued and seen as a cost center rather than a revenue-generating function.

Unfortunately many sales leaders over the years have invested significant resources and investment towards enablement teams and technologies, and for many of the reasons discussed in this book, they have failed to see a clear return—tainting their view of the function. As a result, many sales leaders lean heavily on their front-line managers to fill the "enablement" gap.

When faced with tough cost-cutting initiatives, most sales leaders will prioritize saving their revenue operations leader over their enablement counterpart. Just look at the recent wave of layoffs—how many talented enablement professionals have been affected?

Or consider the struggle to secure budgets for enablement platforms. Many companies would rather throw another SDR at their revenue problems than invest in a solution that could elevate the entire sales team.

It's a harsh but very real reality. And one that I'm determined to help change.

Getting off the content creation hamster wheel

Currently, many enablement professionals are trapped in a content delivery rat race. They're constantly reacting to urgent requests, shifting priorities, and the insatiable demand for more content. "New priority! We need this training right now!" Sound familiar? It's no wonder so many enablement professionals feel perpetually behind. This constant firefighting leaves little time for strategic thinking or analysis.

Without clear visibility into reps' day-to-day activities and performance, or time prioritized to deep-dive and analyze what's working and what's not, it's difficult to identify true skill gaps and demonstrate the value of enablement initiatives.

Enablement professionals often rely on gut instinct, but without concrete data, it's hard to justify prioritizing skill development over creating the latest battlecard or pitch deck.

This reactive cycle needs to change. Imagine a future where instead of saying, "I *think* we could improve sales performance by...," one confidently declares: "Here's the precise performance gap, and here's *exactly* what we need to do to close it."

As AI automates tedious tasks like content delivery and management, enablement professionals will be free to focus on higher-value activities, including:

- **Proactive gap identification**: Use insights to uncover risky patterns, hidden skill gaps, and performance barriers *before* they affect revenue.

- **Holistic enablement strategy**: Design comprehensive programs that address the root causes of performance issues.

- **Data-driven optimization**: Analyze performance data to identify trends, measure content effectiveness, and personalize the learning experience.

The future of enablement is a symphony of human and machine: leveraging data, expertise, and human touch to create a thriving learning culture.

The new strategic partner: sales performance architect

In today's rapidly accelerating landscape, particularly with the rise of AI, sales leaders must fundamentally rethink how to build successful teams—and who they need by their side.

To survive, the role of sales enablement must evolve. While many sales leaders still perceive enablement as primarily focused on training and content management, this view no longer reflects the function's true potential. To meet the demands of today's complex sales environment, enablement must be recognized—and practiced—as a more strategic, data-driven discipline.

> To survive, the role of sales enablement must evolve.

Just as sales leaders turn to revenue operations for strategic go-to-market insights (capacity planning, territory optimization, technology choices, etc.), and call center leaders rely on their operations counterparts, sales leaders need that same level of strategic thinking to optimize their most valuable asset: their people and their individual sales performance.

They need a dedicated partner—**a sales performance architect**—who can holistically identify, and help them address, skill gaps and sales performance roadblocks before they impact the bottom line. This isn't a luxury—it's a necessity.

The sales performance architect is the new strategic partner for sales leadership, and today's enablement professionals are poised to become these architects of tomorrow.

The growth of sales enablement into the sales performance architect role, with its increased focus on data and strategy, mirrors the expansion of skills seen in the growth from Salesforce administrator to revenue operations leader.

The sales performance architect is the new strategic partner for sales leadership, and today's enablement professionals are poised to become these architects of tomorrow.

Salesforce Administrators, often with IT backgrounds, typically begin by meticulously managing user access, configuring settings, and ensuring smooth platform operation. Many master the platform's intricacies, optimize its potential, and then broaden their skill sets to include business analysis and systems thinking. These expanded skills prepare them for roles as revenue operations leaders. Today, many of those early Salesforce administrators, now lead global RevOps teams, orchestrating complex systems and driving strategic growth.

Enablement professionals *can* follow a similar path, leveraging their deep understanding of training, learning methodologies, and performance drivers to architect high-performing organizations. *However*, this evolution requires a fundamental shift, particularly a mindset oriented toward data. The future sales performance architect must possess not only a deep understanding of human psychology and learning science, but also—and critically—expertise in data analytics.

By embracing this strategic, data-driven mindset and developing these essential new skills, enablement professionals can position themselves as indispensable partners to sales leaders, providing data-driven insights, designing transformative learning programs, and driving measurable improvements in sales performance.

> **PRO TIP**

Sharpen your data skills

Embrace a data-driven approach to performance optimization that doesn't rely entirely on other teams. Become a data detective and become really good at collecting and analyzing sales performance data to identify skill gaps and predict future needs.

Add blocks to your calendar on a weekly basis (start with one hour for each):

- **Prioritize the questions you want answers to**: Don't get lost in a sea of data. Start by prioritizing the questions you want answered. Each quarter, take time to identify two to three specific questions you want to explore with your data. For example, start with a question like 'What content do our top-performing new hires use most during onboarding?' Then, analyze ramp performance data, content analytics, and gather qualitative feedback through interviews or surveys to find the answers.

- **Deep dive into your CRM**: Don't just pull basic reports. Master your CRM or other tool's reporting functionality, and explore the depths of your CRM data to uncover hidden patterns in sales performance. Look for correlations between rep activities (emails, calls, meetings) and outcomes (deals won/lost).

- **Master data visualization**: Familiarize yourself with data visualization tools, starting with the dashboards available in your CRM. Charts and graphs can uncover hidden trends and insights that might be missed in spreadsheets, making it easier to identify areas for improvement.

- **Accelerate your data analysis with AI**: If you have a company-approved AI tool, experiment with using it to analyze your data. Many of these tools allow you to upload spreadsheets and ask questions in plain English, such as 'What are the top three factors correlated with high deal close rates?' This can save you time and help you uncover hidden patterns in your data."

Armed with data and AI-powered insights, you'll have the evidence needed to drive strategic decisions and demonstrate the undeniable effect of enablement on revenue growth, earning you a real seat at the table.

The human touch

Does this book suggest that the future of enablement is purely data-driven and delivered asynchronously? Should we abandon Zoom training altogether due to the perceived inefficiencies? No. But those sessions will—and should—look different than they do today, with a laser focus being placed on motivation and engagement.

As automation proliferates and reps gain easier, on-demand access to training and knowledge, the value of human connection will soar. In-person interactions will become even more crucial for fostering engagement, inspiration, and a sense of community.

Think of instructor-led training (whether live on Zoom or in person) as prime real estate for human connection. These sessions will become less about delivering information and more about:

- **Igniting inspiration**: motivating reps and fostering a shared sense of purpose.

- **Cultivating collaboration**: creating opportunities for peer-to-peer learning, coaching, and knowledge sharing.

- **Deepening relationships**: building trust and rapport among team members.

While AI can automate many tasks, it can't replicate the empathy, creativity, and critical thinking that humans bring to the table. Here's where the enablement professionals' expertise will remain essential:

- **Coaching and mentoring**: providing personalized guidance and support, even with on-demand resources available.

- **Building relationships and trust**: connecting with employees on a personal level and understanding their unique challenges.

- **Facilitating collaboration and knowledge sharing**: creating a culture of learning and community.

The result? A workforce that's constantly learning, adapting, and exceeding expectations. Sales teams will become more agile, closing deals more quickly, and building stronger customer relationships.

Enablement is a team sport: Five tips for building buy-in across your org

We've explored the exciting potential of enablement to evolve into a more strategic role. Now, let's translate that vision into action.

Building a world-class enablement program is a team sport. It requires a unified team, all rowing in the same direction. It demands alignment from leadership, the empowerment of reps, and a shared culture of continuous learning.

Without buy-in from senior leadership and front-line managers, enablement programs will struggle to gain traction and deliver results. Organizations need leadership, especially the GTM leadership and CEO backing, to view enablement as a strategic initiative—and support it. This buy-in is equally crucial from sales reps as well.

The good news? Getting buy-in might be a little easier in 2025 and beyond. A recent Salesforce survey of hundreds of sales leaders across 27 countries revealed a surprising finding: The top tactic for growth in 2025 is "improving sales enablement and training." This prioritization even surpasses targeting new markets or optimizing product offerings.

In this section, we'll explore the practical steps you can take today to secure buy-in and build a foundation for lasting success. While these tips are primarily directed toward enablement professionals and sales leaders, they're relevant to anyone interested in improving their organization's sales performance. Consider the following:

1. Influence leadership through insights

Would you like to influence your organization's strategy? No matter your role, become a trusted source of field insights for your leadership team. By regularly sharing data-driven observations and recommendations, you can demonstrate your value and drive meaningful change.

A simple step? Listen to more calls.

It's an easier task to do than most people think. Many conversation intelligence tools have mobile apps, allowing you to listen to a call on the go. Listening to your top reps is especially important. By capturing and analyzing what your top 20% are doing differently, you can unlock the secrets to their success and empower the remaining 80% to achieve similar results.

PRO TIP

Listen to calls

Have every person on your enablement team commit to listening to one to five sales calls per week. At max, that's three hours per week (they can listen at 1.5x speed), or a little over 5% of their time, dedicated to staying apprised of what's happening in the field.

Bring the insights together in a weekly email to your sales leadership with a few trends you heard and any suggested enablement. A few things to include would be:

- **Key competitive insights:** Did you hear any new competitive intel?
- **Trends:** Are certain objections coming up more often?
- **Toughest objection of the week:** Did any objection kill a deal immediately or stall the process?

Make sure to include the link to the call (even better, the link to the referenced snippet) to make it easier for people to participate and learn. You'll earn stripes with your sales leadership and get the clarity and confidence you need to drive the best enablement program possible.

2. Shadow your reps

In Chapter Four, we discussed how shadowing your reps can help you uncover productivity killers.

It's also an excellent way to identify enablement gaps. In the future, your reps' AI enablement assistant will know all about each rep's individual preferences and needs. But until then, they have their managers, first and foremost. And then, they have you - in enablement, marketing and revenue operations.

Unless you're supporting a very small team, it's unlikely you'll get to know each individual rep and their strengths at the same level as their manager (which is why partnership with front-line managers is so important).

But you can gain valuable knowledge by immersing yourself in their world. Beyond listening to calls, consider shadowing one or two of your reps once a week.

When I first took over Salesforce at RealtyShares, I didn't understand our loan originators' prospecting process. The existing CRM implementation was clearly not being used, and frankly, it looked overly complicated. So, I asked five of our reps if I could shadow them for an hour each. I wanted to observe how each of them did their job and why their existing workflow (outside of the CRM) mattered. They were more than happy to invite me into their world, and the insights I gained were invaluable. I was able to build the things they were asking for (or simplify the existing processes), and in return, they served as valuable champions to reinforce the new solutions with their team.

If you're struggling to identify even one rep you feel comfortable shadowing, it suggests an area for improvement. Building that level of trust with your sales team is essential for effective enablement, especially if you haven't carried a quota yourself.

PRO TIP

Shadow reps to understand their workflows

One of the best ways to gain insights into a reps' needs is to observe them in action.

- **Start with a casual conversation**: A simple way to demonstrate curiosity is to ask them to show you their go-to prospecting emails and discuss their approach. What works well? Why do they take that approach? What are some of the best responses they've gotten? You'll be surprised how eager reps are to share their expertise.

- **Shadow their workflow**: Ask if you can join them (in person or virtually) as they prepare for their day. The key here is to observe how they *actually work*. Observe how they prioritize accounts, conduct research, and craft their outreach. Similarly, shadow them as they prepare for important calls. What resources do they use? Are they reviewing their Opportunity? Are they using their own note-taking app? Are they going back and revisiting their last call? What additional research are they doing?

- **Focus on understanding, not judging**: Make it clear that your goal is to learn what makes them effective, not to evaluate their performance.

Soak it all in.

By observing your reps' workflows firsthand, you'll gain valuable insights into their needs, challenges, and preferences. And all of that informs your enablement strategy and content creation efforts.

3. Embrace just-in-time feedback

Similarly, embrace real feedback from your reps.

It always surprises me to hear how few of our customers consistently get real, tangible feedback from their reps. I often ask Spekit customers the honest question: On a scale of 1-10, how would your best rep rate your enablement/onboarding/content? The most common reaction is almost always sheepishness and shame—they don't know exactly, but it's likely not great. And when I ask them when is the last time they surveyed the team to get an answer, it's usually been at least six months.

Feedback and data are a gift. There are numerous ways to gather feedback, from champion groups and one-on-ones to informal coffee chats, quick Slack messages to trusted advisors ("What did you think of that enablement session? Please be honest."), and even formal surveys. And I know what you're thinking, I don't like surveys, either. However, I do deeply value feedback. And when done intentionally (and kept bite-sized), surveys can be successful.

PRO TIP

Gather feedback with bite-sized surveys

Gain valuable insights into your onboarding process and identify potential enablement gaps by conducting short surveys with new hires. For example, on their two-month anniversaries, ask three simple questions:

- What was the most difficult part of learning your new role?

- What processes caused the most confusion?

- Is there any training or enablement that was missing from your onboarding that would've made you feel more confident, more quickly?

Remember to keep the surveys to a max of five questions. I like to set the expectation that any survey should take under two minutes to fill out.

These surveys provide valuable feedback to refine your onboarding program and ensure you're creating content that truly meets your team's needs. Consider conducting similar surveys whenever you're working on your content strategy, whether it's an audit, a cleanup effort, or the implementation of a new content system.

4. Unleash the power of your sales champions

Tap into your team's collective wisdom.

Go beyond simple shadowing and create a **high-impact task force**. Imagine a powerhouse team of your best sales minds working together to elevate the entire organization.

Call it a sales champions group, a center of excellence, or whatever resonates with your team—the name matters less than the purpose. This group should be composed of your best front-line managers, sales leadership, and a diverse group of influential reps, including both top performers and those non-believers you need to win over. Their insights will be invaluable in shaping your enablement strategy and driving adoption.

This group's mission? Make your reps unstoppable. The group's purpose? To uncover, share, and amplify winning strategies. This isn't about planning projects; it's about harnessing your best reps' collective wisdom to fuel continuous improvement.

Nothing is more motivating than seeing what top performers are doing to achieve success.

By empowering your sales champions to identify, share, and amplify these winning strategies, you'll create a culture of continuous learning and drive exceptional results.

PRO TIP

Develop a sales excellence program

To foster a culture of continuous improvement and knowledge sharing, create an exclusive program.

- **Fuel the fire:** Name it something exciting and set special criteria required to join. You want to create FOMO (fear of missing out), similar to President's Club, so that the best of the best want to join and participate.

- **Facilitate collaboration**: Create a dedicated Slack channel for ongoing collaboration and knowledge sharing.

- **Incentive excellence**: Allocate a quarterly budget for a prize (that the group votes on) to recognize the member with the most influential contributions. Depending on your organization's size, that could even include getting the chance to meet one-on-one over a lunch or dinner with a senior executive or the chief executive officer.

- **Schedule monthly power sessions**: Use these sessions to:

    - **Uncover gems**: Share key insights on performance gaps and areas for improvement.

    - **Gather intel**: Collect valuable feedback directly from reps and managers.

    - **Amplify best practices**: Showcase winning strategies and replicate success across the team.

    - **Generate excitement**: Socialize upcoming enablement initiatives and get early buy-in.

    - **Document and share**: Capture and disseminate best practices, like a rep's unique approach to building a winning business case. Turn these insights into templates and resources accessible to the entire team.

5. Lead through your leaders: repetition and reinforcement

All the efforts we've discussed so far culminate in this crucial step: **leading through your leaders**.

Enablement is not a one-and-done activity; it requires ongoing reinforcement and support—we all know this. The challenge is in finding creative ways to reintroduce important concepts in various formats and contexts over time. And who better to champion this reinforcement than your sales leaders?

Do you do extensive planning for your sales kickoff? You should spend just as much time planning for post kickoff reinforcement as you do for the sessions themselves. Remember: You're up against the goldfish memory. You're guaranteed to see better retention and knowledge absorption from your team if you repeat key messages often.

Enable managers to reinforce key learnings in their one-on-ones and team meetings. Create a Slack channel where your reps can share examples of putting a new skill, content, or product sale in motion. Offer prizes and gamify it. Work with your sales managers and executive team to reinforce enablement in meetings and communications. The list of opportunities for reinforcement goes on, but you need a plan to hold yourself and your teams accountable.

PRO TIP

For sales leaders and executives: How to champion enablement from the top

Here's how you can champion enablement and reinforce its value:

- **Lead by example:** Actively engage with enablement content and tools yourself. Share your experiences and demonstrate its value to your team.

- **Integrate into meetings:** Dedicate time in your weekly sales meetings to highlight key enablement resources or discuss best practices. Use real-world examples to illustrate how enablement translates to success.

- **Recognize and reward:** Publicly acknowledge reps who effectively leverage enablement resources in their deals. Celebrate their wins and showcase the positive effect of their efforts.

- **Provide feedback:** Encourage open communication and feedback about your enablement program. Actively solicit input from your team to ensure its relevance and effectiveness.

- **Collaborate with enablement**: Work closely with your enablement team to align initiatives with sales goals and priorities. Provide insights into the challenges your reps face and the resources they need to succeed.

A little reinforcement goes a long way toward driving adoption and creating a culture of continuous learning. By actively supporting enablement, you invest in your team's success and pave the way for greater revenue growth.

The infinite possibilities

I could dedicate many more chapters to exploring how AI will change the enablement org structure, content strategy, skills training, such as role-playing, and the process of designing effective onboarding, but this book is already double the length I intended! (Not so bite- sized after all). Fortunately, many excellent resources are available on these subjects.

While the prospect of significant change can feel overwhelming, you have the opportunity to embrace the unknown and transform your organizations by focusing on incremental improvement—getting just 1% better each day. Every step you take brings us closer to a future where every employee is empowered to reach their full potential.

The future of enablement is being written now, and you have an important role to play.

Don't wait for the perfect platform or the ideal strategy. Even without a fully implemented Just-In-Time Enablement platform, you can take practical steps and start experimenting with AI to make your enablement more effective and prepare your company for future success.

Here's a quick cheat sheet summarizing the Pro Tips discussed in this book:

Pro Tips for navigating the future of enablement

1. Avoid the "shiny object" trap.
2. Identify hidden productivity killers.
3. Add content shortcuts in your tool.
4. Make data hygiene a priority.
5. Start shifting to an everboarding model.
6. Train reps on how to get better answers from AI.
7. Embrace bite-sized content today.
8. Create a repeatable change enablement process.
9. Understand change management best practices.
10. Embrace AI-powered content curation tools.
11. Sharpen your data skills.
12. Listen to sales calls.
13. Shadow reps to understand their workflows.
14. Gather feedback with bite-sized surveys.
15. Develop a sales excellence program.
16. Champion enablement from the top.

CONCLUSION

The clock is ticking: adapt or get left behind

Thank you for joining me on this exploration into the future.

Turns out, the ending of the RealtyShares story is a poignant one. A couple of years after I left, the company folded because it ran out of time. While the reasons were complex, it serves as a stark reminder that even with innovative solutions, timing and execution are critical.

Ultimately, in the race for success, speed is the ultimate weapon. In today's hyper-competitive market, companies can't afford to stand still. The need to adapt, optimize, and empower your workforce has never been more urgent. The future belongs to those who act decisively and equip their teams to learn and execute at lightning speed. Your competitors won't wait for you to catch up, nor will your prospects.

The question isn't if you need to rethink your approach to enablement, but how *quickly* can you transform.

But it's not the fear of the latter that motivates me. It's about seizing the extraordinary possibilities of what's ahead —we're at the start of a new era, one where technology and human potential converge to unlock unprecedented levels of performance and revenue growth.

The future of enablement is bright, filled with a more engaging, effective, and personalized learning experience that's focused on tangible outcomes: increased revenue, improved sales performance, and a learning experience that your reps genuinely enjoy.

While this book may end here, your journey of exploration and discovery has just begun. Embrace the challenge, experiment fearlessly, and continue to learn and adapt. The future of enablement is in your hands.

Keep it *Simple*, yet *Spektacular*.

For more tips and educational content, visit **www.justintimeenablement.com**

Acknowledgments

This book is a testament to my belief in the power of enablement to unlock human potential. As I reflect on my journey, I'm grateful for the challenges that inspired me and the opportunity to make a lasting effect on the way people learn and work. While pouring my life into this vision hasn't been easy, I wouldn't have it any other way.

First, I want to thank my wonderful book team. Kelly, thank you for your patience through countless revisions, and Jenny, for bringing this book to life visually. I couldn't have done it without you both! Katy, my amazing right-hand woman, thank you for keeping my world running smoothly and for ensuring this book made it to the finish line. And Tracy, for stepping in to support as well!

My deepest gratitude to my beta readers: Ali, Gina, Chris, John, Whitney, Michelle, Tommy, Seth, Freddy, Nav, Brett, Jonathan, Mama, Sean, Jason, Jackie, and Jeff. Your radical candor and insightful feedback shaped this book. And thank you, Sheevaun, for the goldfish memory reference!

To Zari, my cofounder - we took this leap of faith together and I'm so proud of what we've built. Spekit wouldn't exist without you. I hope to make you proud as I carry the torch forward.

True innovation requires those willing to embrace the unknown. To our first twenty employees—Najam, Hammad, Jeff, Maaz, Shariq, Abdullah, Shehzad, Sarmad, Elle, David, Freddy, Ryan, Courtney, Sarah, Christian, Rees, Sadaf, Iqra, Jason and Jacob—thank you for believing in this dream when it was just that, a dream.

To Jason, Paul, Seth, Jackie, Larkin, Kate, Lucia, Mike, and every other member of the Spekit team, past and present, thank you for your tenacity and commitment to delivering a *Simple*, yet *Spektacular* experience. As Zari always said, time is our most precious asset, and we deeply appreciate you dedicating so much of yours to building this company and bringing this vision to life.

To Dan, Brett, Natty, Mallun, Leyla, Jaclyn, Roseanne, Brian, Victoria, and all our investors – your belief in me and in this vision has been nothing short of incredible. Thank you for your support and trust.

To our earliest customers and believers who put their faith in us, even when we were still finding our footing, thank you. Your willingness to take a chance and be pioneers alongside us has helped shape everything we've built.

David, my rock, thank you for making me laugh every day and your endless love and support.

And finally, thank you to the rest of my phenomenal network of friends and family who have patiently listened to me talk about Just-In-Time Enablement and Spekit nonstop for the past eight years. You've been my constant source of strength and encouragement through good times and bad. Thank you for always lifting me up and understanding my hectic life.

And to the enablement community—the practitioners, the thought leaders, the learners, and the innovators—thank you. Your passion for this field is contagious, and it's been a privilege to learn alongside you.

LEGAL DISCLAIMER:

This book reflects the author's personal experiences and opinions. References to companies, products, and individuals are for illustrative purposes only and do not imply endorsement, sponsorship, or affiliation.

All trademarks mentioned in this publication are the property of their respective owners. Their inclusion does not imply endorsement or affiliation.